JONATHAN EDWARDS
ON THE EXPERIENCE OF BEAUTY

Jonathan Edwards Classic Studies Series

The Young Jonathan Edwards
William Sparkes Morris
With a new foreword by Kenneth Minkema

Jonathan Edwards, Pastor
Patricia Tracy

Jonathan Edwards's Moral Thought and Its British Context
Norman Fiering

Beauty and Sensibility in the Thought of Jonathan Edwards
Roland A. Delattre

Religion and the American Mind
Alan Heimert

Samuel Hopkins and the New Divinity Movement
Joseph A. Conforti

Edwards on the Will: A Century of Anglican Theological Debate
Allen C. Guelzo

Jonathan Edwards: The First Critical Biography, 1889
Alexander V. G. Allen

Jonathan Edwards and the Covenant of Grace
Carl W. Bogue

The Philosophy of Jonathan Edwards: From His Private Notebook
Edited by Harvey G. Townsend

Jonathan Edwards: Theologian of the Heart
Harold P. Simonson

Future volumes are forthcoming. For current updates see http://edwards.yale.edu.

JONATHAN EDWARDS
ON THE EXPERIENCE OF BEAUTY

LOUIS J. MITCHELL

WIPF & STOCK • Eugene, Oregon

Wipf and Stock Publishers
199 W 8th Ave, Suite 3
Eugene, OR 97401

Jonathan Edwards on the Experience of Beauty
By Mitchell, Louis J.
Copyright©2003 by Mitchell, Louis J.
ISBN 13: 978-1-5326-0359-4
Publication date 7/29/2016
Previously published by Princeton Theological Seminary, 2003

The Jonathan Edwards Classic Studies Series

The Jonathan Edwards Center at Yale University is pleased to offer this volume, in grateful cooperation with Wipf & Stock Publishers, as part of its mission to encourage ongoing research into and readership of one of America's most original thinkers and one of its most significant historical and cultural figures. As much as the Edwards Center is devoted to presenting Edwards's own writings in a comprehensive and authoritative online format, we also see providing secondary resources as vital to supporting an ongoing understanding of Edwards's extensive and varied corpus, which can be accessed at http://edwards.yale.edu.

Writings about Edwards's life, thought, and legacy continue to accumulate from authors representing a broad range of disciplines and agendas. Within the voluminous secondary literature, the Edwards Center recognizes the importance of insuring that certain key works—which sadly have gone out of print but yet remain in demand—are available for new generations coming to the study of Edwards and are recognized for their worth. These monographs represent some of the very best and most pioneering studies of Edwards, his times, and his influence, from scholars over the past half century and more. Indeed, these works not only greatly influenced the study of Edwards but American history in general. We hope these landmark studies, ranging from biography to intellectual and social history to philosophy and theology, continue to be sources of inquiry and inspiration for decades to come.

Harry S. Stout
Director
The Jonathan Edwards Center
Yale University

Contents

FOREWORD	vii
ACKNOWLEDGMENTS AND DEDICATION	viii
INTRODUCTION	ix
I THE LANGUAGE OF BEAUTY	**1**
The Vocabulary of Beauty	1
The Beauty of Love	5
Beauty and the Trinity	10
Beauty and Glory	12
II THE EXPERIENCE OF BEAUTY	**17**
A Sense of the Heart	18
Religious Knowledge	20
A Sense of the Spirit	27
Beauty Perceived	29
III THE MANIFESTATIONS OF BEAUTY	**31**
Beauty Incarnate	31
Excellency of Christ	31
"Proportioned Christians"	41
Corporate Beauty	43
The Beauty of Order	46
The Beauty of Union	49
"One Cannot Subsist Alone"	51
IV SIGNS OF BEAUTY	**55**
Religious Affections	55
Negative Signs	59
Positive Signs	62

V	Cases of Beauty	75
	A Faithful Narrative	75
	The Case of Abigail Hutchinson	77
	The Case of Phoebe Bartlet	78
	The Case of Jonathan Edwards	80
	Some Thoughts on the Revival	90
	The Case of Sarah Edwards	90
	The Case of David Brainerd	94
	Conclusion	105
	Bibliography	109
	Index	113

Foreword

Jonathan Edwards on the Experience of Beauty was first published in 2003 in Princeton Theological Seminary's niche series Studies in Reformed Theology and History. Since then, the literature on Edwards and beauty has grown considerably. In that context Mitchell's book has received a small but steady stream of attention, thus meriting its republication here. In the original "Editor's Foreword," E. David Willis wrote, "Dr. Mitchell is one of the group who over the years have conspired in Edwardsian things with Richard R. Niebuhr at Harvard." Knowing Willis's affection for the theology department at Harvard, I am certain he used "conspired" in a playful sense. However, etymologically speaking, "conspired" as "breathed together" is also an apt way to understand the development of "the group." Mitchell, Sang H. Lee, Krister Sairsingh, and other Niebuhr students learned much from observing their teacher think through Edwards' positions. In time they joined Niebuhr in ruminating over Edwards' writings. Careful study of Mitchell's book will take readers straight to the heart of Edwards' theology, revealing his aesthetic approach to ethics along the way.

Stephen D. Crocco
Yale University

Acknowledgments and Dedication

I acknowledge a debt of gratitude to Richard R. Niebuhr for his insight, grace, and kindness in guiding the dissertation upon which this book is based and to David Willis for the opportunity to publish this study in Princeton Theological Seminary's monograph series Studies in Reformed Theology and History.

I dedicate this book to my sister Betty Lou, who has always lived a life in God's beauty; to Steve, you know what you did; and to Jonathan, Jennifer, Elizabeth, and Leah, who grew up with the secret (no longer) family pass code: "Jonathan Edwards."

Introduction

Beauty as a theological idea is getting a lot of attention these days. But beauty—as in beauty of the Lord—is not a new concept. Since the time of Augustine, theologians have argued that God is beautiful and that God's redemptive plan for the world unfolds along the lines of the revelation of divine beauty. Catholic theologian Hans Urs von Balthasar has built a modern "aesthetic theology" around the concept of "the glory of the Lord."[1] Increasingly, theologians are pointing to Jonathan Edwards (1703–58) as the first Protestant theologian of beauty. Significant works by Roland Delattre, Norman Fiering, and Sang Lee have provided the language, intellectual background, and philosophical foundation of what is now understood as a pervasive theme in Edwards' writings.[2]

Building on their contributions, this book examines the subjective or experiential dimensions of Edwards' idea of beauty, exploring not only the Trinitarian foundation of God's beauty but also how, according to Edwards, God's beauty is experienced by humans. It has been noted by others that Edwards understood God's beauty as displayed in nature and incarnated in

---

1. See his *The Glory of the Lord: A Theological Aesthetics*, vol. 1 (San Francisco: Ignatius Press, 1982).

2. Roland Delattre, *Beauty and Sensibility in the Thought of Jonathan Edwards: An Essay in Aesthetics and Theological Ethics* (New Haven: Yale University Press, 1968); Norman Fiering, *Jonathan Edwards's Moral Thought and Its British Context* (Chapel Hill: University of North Carolina Press, 1981); and Sang Hyun Lee, *The Philosophical Theology of Jonathan Edwards*. (Princeton: Princeton University Press, 1988).

Jesus Christ.³ However, my study addresses how humans existentially, personally and really, connect with God's beauty. To quote C. S. Lewis, "We do not want merely to *see* beauty. . . . We want something else . . . to be united with the beauty we see, to pass into it, to receive it into our selves, to bathe in it, to become part of it."⁴ For Edwards, this union takes place through what he calls "the sense of the heart." This experience produces a manifestation of beauty in people's lives, individually and corporately; stated boldly, beauty reveals an ethic for living a moral and holy life.

Jonathan Edwards on the Experience of Beauty demonstrates how the language of beauty is the solution to what was for him the most important issue of his time—the "nature of true religion."⁵ What is a genuine experience of God supposed to look like? How should such an experience be authenticated in one's life? Edwards' answer to both questions is "beauty." Beauty is the very structure of genuine religious experience.⁶

---

3. On Edwards and the beauty of nature, see Richard Cartwright Austin, *Beauty of the Lord: Awakening the Senses* (Atlanta: John Knox, 1988). On beauty and the Incarnation, see Louis Joseph Mitchell, "The Experience of Beauty in the Thought of Jonathan Edwards" (ThD thesis, Harvard University, 1995) 81–83.

4. C. S. Lewis, *The Weight of Glory* (New York: HarperCollins, 2001) 42.

5. *The Works of Jonathan Edwards*, vol. 2, *Religious Affections* (New Haven: Yale University Press) 84. This series of Edwards' works, edited by Perry Miller (vols. 1 and 2), John E. Smith (vols. 3–9), and most recently by Harry S. Stout (vols. 10–22), will be cited throughout as "Yale," followed by the volume number.

6. Since my book was published, there have been a number of works on Edwards and beauty. See, for example, Louis J. Mitchell, "The Theological Aesthetics of Jonathan Edwards," *Theology Today* 64 (2007) 36–46. Michael J. McClymond and Gerald R. McDermott devote an entire chapter to aesthetics in their *Theology of Jonathan Edwards* (New York: Oxford University Press, 2012) 93–101. Edwards' idea of beauty has also become important in the broader field of theological aesthetics. See, for example, William A. Dyrness, *Poetic Theology: God and the Poetics of Everyday Life* (Grand Rapids: Eerdmans, 2011) 14, and Belden C. Lane, *Ravished by Beauty: The Surprising Legacy of Reformed Spirituality* (New York: Oxford University Press, 2011) 193.

I

The Language of Beauty

Edwards understood the idea of beauty as a complex of related ideas. For him, beauty existed in many forms and degrees. He applied that range of meanings in a number of diverse ways throughout his philosophical theology and the practice of his ministry. Indeed, Thomas Schafer has stated that the influence of such ideas as excellency and beauty on Edwards' theology cannot be overemphasized.[3]

THE VOCABULARY OF BEAUTY

In 1723 Edwards began a series of entries in a private notebook he entitled "The Mind." The first entry, originally a separate miscellany, is a lengthy discussion of *Excellency*.[4] It is in the exposition of the idea of excellency that one discovers the fundamentals of Edwards' understanding of beauty, what might be termed the vocabulary of his language of beauty. The terms *excellency* and *beauty* functioned within a particular range of meanings in philosophical and Puritan writings. Such terms were common in seventeenth- and eighteenth-century theology. In the first entry of "The Mind," *excellency* is the broader term encompassing, among others, such concepts as beauty, holiness, and greatness. *Beauty* is thus a synonym for excellency. For our purposes, the terms *excellency* and *beauty* may be used interchangeably; therefore, throughout this study, *excellency* may be read as *beauty*. As Edwards

---

[3] Thomas Schafer, editor's introduction to Yale 13, p. 54.
[4] It is under the heading of "Excellency" that Edwards begins his first entry in "The Mind." The text of "The Mind" is found in Yale 6 pp. 332–393. On the dating of "The Mind" see pp. 8, 9, 28, and 29. Thomas Schafer dates this first entry as September–October, 1723. See Yale 13, table 2, p. 92.

wrote in a later entry, "Excellence, to put it in other words, is that which is beautiful and lovely."[5]

In the first entry of "The Mind," Edwards writes:

> There has nothing been more without a definition than excellency, although it be what we are more concerned with than anything else whatsoever. Yea, we are concerned with nothing else. But what is excellency? Wherein is one thing excellent and another evil, one beautiful and another deformed?[6]

In these introductory comments, Edwards, demonstrating his scientific and empirical curiosity, probes the definition of beauty. In doing so he links himself with the inquiry of philosophers and theologians from antiquity through the Enlightenment. Edwards accepts a traditional definition of beauty as regularity or proportionality; but he is not satisfied with that definition. He wants to know why beauty is what it is:

> Some have said that all excellency is harmony, symmetry or proportion; but they have not yet explained it. We would know why proportion is more excellent than disproportion, that is, why proportion is pleasant to the mind and disproportion unpleasant. Proportion is a thing that may be explained yet further.[7]

Edwards' response to his own inquiry is that beauty in its most elementary form consists in a certain relatedness between entities. This relatedness involves a similarity or likeness of one kind or another. He succinctly states that "excellency therefore seems to consist in equality." Later in the same entry he states, "all beauty consists in similarness, or identity of relation."[8]

For Edwards there is a kind of objectivity to beauty. Beauty is relational in nature. Beauty must therefore display some sort of relatedness between entities. Here the reader is introduced to the first of a series of terms which comprise and elucidate Edwards' understanding of beauty. For, says Edwards, the relation of simple equality or exact correspondence "may be called simple beauty—all other beauties and excellencies may be resolved into it."[9] Circles with equal radii, triangles with equal sides, lines with equidistant points portray what Edwards calls *simple beauty*. Anything that corresponds exactly to another thing shows forth beauty at its most basic level.

---

[5] "The Mind," Yale 6, p. 344.
[6] Ibid., p. 332.
[7] Ibid.
[8] Ibid., pp. 332, 334.
[9] Ibid., p. 333.

Another level of beauty is portrayed in what Edwards terms *complex beauty*. Simply stated, "proportion is complex beauty." In complex beauty, the relatedness goes beyond mere equality into a more sophisticated "identity of relation." Edwards illustrates with another geometric example: points on a straight line having distances with the ratio of one half the distance from the preceding point (point A four inches from point B which is two inches from point C, etc.) cannot be said to be equal in distance. However, the distances are proportionately related. They are harmonized into a more complex whole. They thereby exhibit complex beauty.[10]

In "The Mind," Edwards explicates an important characteristic of complex beauty, anticipating terminology he uses in other writings. He states that "particular disproportions sometimes greatly add to the general beauty, and must necessarily be in order to a more universal proportion."[11] Beauty can be *intensified* through the harmonization of disproportions, inequalities, or irregularities. This intensification of beauty is accomplished through a conjunction of diverse, even antithetical, qualities. The more inequalities and irregularities that can be conjoined into a proportional relation, the greater and more intensified is the beauty. The human body, for example, exhibits a conjunction of diverse shapes which make a whole, more intensely beautiful, entity. Edwards does not use the term *conjunction* in this entry of "The Mind." However, as we shall see, he does use the term in other writings, for example his "Personal Narrative" and "The Excellency of Christ," to show such a harmonization toward a more universal proportion.

Music provides a helpful illustration of what Edwards means. Voices singing in unison portray a simple beauty of equality, each individual voice singing the same notes. However, a choir singing in four-part harmony evidences a more sophisticated beauty. Although the various voices are not singing the same notes, the notes are proportionately related through harmony. The more sophisticated the relations, the more intensified the beauty becomes. Thus the music produced by a large choir, accompanied by a full orchestra, performing Beethoven's Ninth Symphony, may be said to be intensely beautiful.

The complex beauty of proportionality can be evident in a number of ways. It is portrayed in the symmetry and proportionality of geometric figures, in the harmony of music, in the related shapes of the human face or body, or in the consistent strokes of graceful penmanship. Indeed it is complex beauty that defines for Edwards the scope of what he calls *natural beauty*:

---

[10] Ibid.
[11] Ibid., p. 335.

that sort of beauty which is called "natural," as of vines, plants, trees, etc., consists of a very complicated harmony; and all the motions and tendencies and figures of bodies in the universe are done according to proportion, and therein is their beauty.[12]

In an essay entitled "Beauty of the World," Edwards writes:

> 'Tis very probable that wonderful suitableness of green for the grass and plants, the blue of the sky, the white of the clouds, the colors of flowers, consists in a complicated proportion that these colors make one with another, either in the magnitude of the rays, the number of vibrations that are caused in the optic nerve, or some other way. So there is a great suitableness between the objects of different senses, as between sounds, colors, and smells—as between the colors of the woods and flowers, and the smell and the singing of birds—which 'tis probable consist in a certain proportion of the vibrations that are made in the different organs . . . [W]hat an infinite number of such-like beauties is there in that one thing, the light; and how complicated an harmony and proportion is it probable belongs to it.[13]

All of the various kinds of beauty which we have noted thus far fit into a larger classification which Edwards calls *secondary beauty*. Secondary beauty is the beauty of equality, harmony, symmetry, proportion, etc., in the material world. Edwards says that secondary beauty

> is found even in inanimate things: which consists in a mutual consent and agreement of different things in form, manner, quantity and visible end and design; called by the various names of regularity, order, uniformity, symmetry, proportion, harmony, etc.[14]

Secondary beauty appears in immaterial things as well. Edwards says that there is beauty in a well-ordered society which is like the regularity of a beautiful building. Wisdom is beautiful in that it consists in a "united tendency of thoughts, ideas and volitions, to a general purpose." Similarly, justice "consists in the agreement of different things that have relation to one another, in nature, manner, and measure: and therefore is the very same sort of beauty with that uniformity and proportion which is observable in those external and material things that are esteemed beautiful."[15]

---

[12] Ibid., p. 335.
[13] Yale 6, pp. 305, 306.
[14] *The Nature of True Virtue* in Yale 8, pp. 561, 562.
[15] Edwards criticizes both Francis Hutcheson and William Wollaston for basing virtue on these and other forms of secondary beauty. See *Nature of True Virtue*, Yale 8, pp. 568–570.

The Beauty of Love

By definition secondary beauty is inferior (secondary) to another kind of beauty. This higher beauty Edwards calls *primary beauty*. It has been noted that secondary beauty consists in certain relations between objects or natural virtues. Objects displaying secondary beauty are said to *agree* with or *consent* to each other. For example in *The Nature of True Virtue*, it has been noted, Edwards states that secondary beauty "consists in a mutual consent and agreement of different things in form, manner, quantity, and visible end or design; called by the various names of regularity, order, uniformity, symmetry, proportion, harmony, etc." He continues:

> Such is the mutual *agreement* of the various sides of a square, or equilateral triangle, or of a regular polygon. Such is, as it were, the mutual *consent* of the different parts of the periphery of a circle, or surface of a sphere, and of the corresponding parts of an ellipse. Such is the *agreement* of colors, figures, dimensions and distances of the different spots on a chess board. Such is the beauty of the figures in a piece of chintz or brocade. Such is the beautiful proportion of the various parts of a human body, or countenance and such is the sweet mutual *consent* and *agreement* of the various notes of a melodious tune.[16]

The relatedness is a kind of agreement or consent. However, in "The Mind," Edwards notes that the term consent (and agreement also) as related to natural things is borrowed from usage of a different sort:

> When we spake of excellence in bodies we were obliged to borrow the word "consent" from spiritual things. But excellence in and among spirits is, in its prime and proper sense, being's consent to being. There is no other proper consent but that of minds, even of their will; which, when it is of minds towards minds, it is love, and when of minds towards other things it is choice. Wherefore all the primary and original beauty or excellence that is among minds is love, and into this may all be resolved that is found among them.[17]

Consent and agreement are terms that more properly relate to beings capable of choice and love. They are actions of minds exercising volition. It is this kind of relatedness that for Edwards constitutes *primary beauty*. Primary beauty is the beauty of beings in consent or agreement. Indeed, says Edwards, "This is a universal definition of excellency: the consent of being to

---

[16] *Nature of True Virtue*, Yale 8, p. 562. Emphasis added.
[17] "The Mind," #44, Yale 6, p. 362.

being; or being's consent to entity. The more the consent is, and the more extensive, the greater is the excellency."[18]

The highest consent or agreement between beings is *love*. In love, being consents to being in the highest possible way. Thus to experience love is to experience beauty; to be loving is to beautify; to be filled with love is to be beautiful. On the corporate or societal level the beauty of love is manifested in *union*. Edwards writes: "Union is one of the most amiable things, that pertains to human society; yea, 'tis one of the most beautiful and happy things on earth, which indeed makes earth most like heaven."[19]

For Edwards, there is an important relationship between primary and secondary beauty. Secondary beauty mirrors or shadows the beauty of primary beauty. The agreement of equality and proportion in the natural world is a shadow of the agreement or consent of spiritual beings. For example, he writes:

> As bodies, the objects of our external senses, are but the shadows of beings, that harmony wherein consists sensible excellency and beauty is but the shadow of excellency; that is, it is pleasant to the mind because it is a shadow of love. When one thing sweetly harmonizes with another, as the notes in music, the notes are so conformed and have such proportion one to another that they seem to have respect one to another, as if they loved one another.[20]

Several factors of Edwards' philosophical theology come into focus in the relationship between primary and secondary beauty. One can see Edwards' philosophical idealism evident in his neo-Platonic ranking of being. That which is spiritual is higher than that which is physical. The world of mind, spirit, or idea is the more real world. Spirit is more properly being than that which is material.[21]

Secondary beauty is emblematic. It points beyond itself to primary beauty. The natural world and the beauty of the natural world are typological. One of Edwards' private notebooks is devoted to the typology of the natural world. In "Images of Divine Things," Edwards explores some of the dimensions of religious typology. Typology had long been a part of Puritan hermeneutics

---

[18] "The Mind," #1, Yale 6, p. 336.
[19] *An Humble Attempt*, Yale 5, p. 365.
[20] "The Mind," #62, Yale 6, p. 380.
[21] Edwards states: "One of the highest excellencies is love. As nothing else has a proper being but spirits, and as bodies are but the shadow of being, therefore the consent of bodies to one another, and the harmony that is among them, is but the shadow of excellency. The highest excellency, therefore, must be the consent of spirits one to another" ("The Mind," #1, Yale 6, p. 337). On Edwards' philosophical idealism, see George E. Rupp, "The 'Idealism' of Jonathan Edwards," *Harvard Theological Review* 62 (1969).

and homiletic tradition; and Edwards was a master typologist. For Edwards, natural beauty typifies spiritual beauty; secondary beauty typifies primary beauty. Just as the antitype fulfills or completes the type, so does primary beauty fulfill and complete secondary beauty, its shadow.[22]

Happiness or pleasure is the product of the perception of the beauty of consent: "Pleasedness in perceiving being always arises, either from a perception of consent to being in general, or of consent to that being that perceives."[23] Such a perception of consent is an important aspect of Edwards' understanding of happiness. At the end of the first entry in "The Mind," Edwards gives a definition of happiness: "Happiness, strictly, consists in the perception of these three things: of the consent of being to its own being; of its own consent to being; and of being's consent to being."[24] The agreeableness of primary and secondary beauty is pleasurable to any being with the capacity of perception. The perception of beauty, as we shall see, is thus an important activity in Edwards' philosophical theology.

For Edwards, beauty is the very structure of being. Edwards' doctrine of being is that of a relational or dispositional ontology. In the first entry of "The Mind" he writes: "For being, if we examine narrowly, is nothing but proportion." The structure of being is relational in nature; all being is proportionately related. Edwards' relational philosophy of being has been the subject of a number of important studies. Richard R. Niebuhr, for example, states that "the foundation of his philosophy of being, lies in proportionality or in complex, intense beauty."[25]

The notion that the structure of being is that of the beauty of proportion is evidenced by what appears to be something of an innate sense or disposition in human beings toward proportionality:

> How exceedingly apt are we, when we are sitting still and accidentally casting our eye upon some marks or spots in the floor or wall, to be arranging them into regular panels and figures; and if we see a mark out of its place, to be placing of it right by our imagination—and this even while meditating on something else. So we may catch ourselves at

---

[22] *Images of Divine Things* in *Typological Writings*, Yale 11. On Edwards and typology and especially as related to nature, see editor's introduction, Yale 11.
[23] "The Mind," #1, Yale 6, p. 336.
[24] Ibid., p. 338.
[25] Ibid., p. 336; Richard R. Niebuhr, *Streams of Grace: Studies of Jonathan Edwards, Samuel Taylor Coleridge and William James* (Kyoto, Japan: Doshiba University Press, 1983), p. 23. Niebuhr's is one of several important studies in which Edwards' relational or dispositional ontology has been the subject. An older work is that of Douglas J. Elwood, *The Philosophical Theology of Jonathan Edwards* (New York: Columbia University Press, 1960). Sang H. Lee utilizes the same title in his 1988 book.

observing the rule of harmony and regularity in the careless motions of our heads or feet, and when playing with our hands, or walking about the room.[26]

The perception, even unconscious perception, of the beauty of proportionality is inherently pleasing to being:

> Thus, a man may be pleased with the harmony of the notes in a tune and yet know nothing of that proportion or adjustment of the notes, which by the law of nature is the ground of the melody . . . So, a man may be affected and pleased with a beautiful proportion of the features in a face, and yet not know what that proportion is, or what measures, quantities, and distances it consists in.[27]

Human beings delight in the perception of proportionality and regularity. There is agreement and pleasure in the perception of this kind of beauty. Such pleasure, says Edwards, is according to a kind of law of nature which God has established in human beings. For being, itself, according to Edwards, is proportion. Beauty for Edwards, says Sang Lee, "is what the structure of being (i.e. laws and habits) looks like." Thus, says Edwards, "to find out the reason of things in natural philosophy is to find out the proportion of God's activity."[28]

In *The Nature of True Virtue*, Edwards proposes primary beauty as the foundation of all virtue and ethics. There Edwards offers a critique of contemporaneous theories of virtue. He especially challenges the theory of Francis Hutcheson. Hutcheson based ethics, as did Edwards, on an idea of beauty. Hutcheson founded his idea of virtue on the beauty of such relations as justice and uniformity in the midst of diversity. According to Edwards, Hutcheson's idea of virtue was founded on secondary beauty. It was, therefore, based on an inferior kind of beauty. For Edwards, true virtue was that which was founded on the primary beauty of benevolence to being in general. In a direct reference to Hutcheson's notion of beauty, Edwards writes, "Benevolence to being in general, or to being simply considered, is entirely a distinct thing from uniformity in the midst of variety, and is a superior kind of beauty."[29]

Not all beauty may be properly called virtue. It is only primary beauty, the beauty of being that has "*perception* and *will*" which may be so designated.[30]

---

[26] "The Mind," #1, Yale 6, p. 336.
[27] *Nature of True Virtue*, Yale 8, p. 566.
[28] Lee, *Philosophical Theology*, p. 79; "The Mind," #34, Yale 6, p. 353.
[29] *Nature of True Virtue*, Yale 8, p. 571.
[30] Ibid., p. 539.

True virtue is a matter of the will and the heart, involving volition and affections. In the first chapter of *The Nature of True Virtue*, Edwards clarifies and defines the kind of beauty that is virtue. There he makes an important distinction between *general* and *particular beauty*. *Particular beauty* is more limited in scope. Its relations are within a more contained sphere. *General beauty* is beauty of a more universal proportion. Edwards utilizes music to illustrate the difference: "as a few notes in a tune, taken only by themselves, and in their relation one to another, may be harmonious; which when considered with respect to all notes in the tune, or the entire series of sounds they are connected with, may be very discordant and disagreeable."[31] A particular beauty may be beautiful in its limited relations, but not beautiful in a larger or more general context. True virtue must be a beauty which is both primary and general. Such virtue must involve "the *heart* of an intelligent being, that is beautiful by a *general beauty*, or beautiful in a comprehensive view as it is in itself, and as related to everything that it stands in connection with."[32] True virtue must thus relate to being in general or what Edwards calls "being, simply considered."[33]

Another important distinction in Edwards' definition of true virtue is that between the love of *benevolence* and the love of *complacence*. Love which is of complacence "presupposes beauty, for it is no other than delight in beauty; or complacence in the person or being beloved for his beauty."[34] Love of complacence is a love of beauty; the object of such a love is loved on account of, or for the sake of, its beauty. Love of *benevolence*, on the other hand, is a more general goodwill. It is an "affection or propensity of the heart to any being."[35] Love of benevolence does not "necessarily presuppose beauty in its object."[36] Love to being in general allows for a more universal proportion and thus is a higher beauty than is love to particular beings: "True virtue most essentially consists in benevolence to Being in general. Or perhaps to speak more accurately, it is that consent, propensity and union of heart to Being in general, that is immediately exercised in a general good will."[37]

For Edwards the question of the nature of true virtue is not a question of ethics divorced from theology. *The Nature of True Virtue* is a work of theological ethics. In Edwards' philosophical theology, God is what Edwards primarily means by "Being in general." In "The Mind," he writes, "the greater a being is,

---

[31] Ibid., p. 540.
[32] Ibid., p. 540.
[33] Ibid., p. 544.
[34] Ibid., p. 543.
[35] Ibid., p. 542.
[36] Ibid., p. 543.
[37] Ibid., p. 540.

and the more it has of entity, the more will consent to being in general please it. But God is proper entity itself, and those two therefore in him become the same; for so far as a thing consents to being in general, so far it consents to him."[38] Edwards continues, "When we speak of Being in general, we may be understood [to speak] of the divine Being, for he is an infinite being."[39] By benevolence to being in general, Edwards means "chiefly" love to God: "From what has been said, 'tis evident that true virtue most chiefly consists in love to God; the Being of beings, infinitely the greatest and best of beings."[40]

Since God is chiefly understood as Being in general, and since being is proportion, God is most properly beauty and the sum of all beauty:

> God is not only infinitely greater and more excellent than all other being; but he is the head of the universal system of existence; the foundation and fountain of all being and all beauty; from whom all is perfectly derived, and on whom all is most absolutely and perfectly dependent; of whom, and through whom, and to whom is all being and all perfection; and whose being and beauty is as it were the sum and comprehension of all existence and excellence: much more than the sun is the fountain and summary comprehension of all the light and brightness of the day.[41]

Edwards' ontology is decidedly theocentric.

BEAUTY AND THE TRINITY

It has been noted that for Edwards, God is the "fountain and foundation" of all being. Since the structure of being is beauty, God is therefore the sum of all beauty as well. However, God's being poses an interesting problem for Edwards' philosophical system:

> One alone, without any reference to any more, cannot be excellent; for in such a case there can be no manner of relation no way, and therefore, no thing as consent. Indeed, what we call "one" may be excellent, because of a consent of parts, or some consent of those in that being that are distinguished into a plurality some way or other. But in a being that is absolutely without any plurality there cannot be excellency, for there can be no such thing as consent or agreement.[42]

Utter simplicity cannot be beautiful. For in utter simplicity there can be no relation of proportionality or consent to being. For Edwards, being is proportion

---

[38] "The Mind," #1, Yale 6, p. 337.
[39] Ibid., #45, Yale 6, p. 363.
[40] *Nature of True Virtue*, Yale 8, p. 550.
[41] Ibid., p. 551.
[42] "The Mind," #1, Yale 6, p. 337.

and the structure of being is that of beauty. If God is to be Being in general, the source of all being and the source of all beauty, God must be beautiful; that is, God must have proportionality in God's being. Edwards restates the philosophical problem in one of his miscellanies: "[O]ne alone cannot be excellent, inasmuch as, in such case, there can be no consent. Therefore, if God is excellent, there must be a plurality in God; otherwise there can be no consent in him."[43] It is in Edwards' concept of God as Trinity that the proportionality, consent, and therefore beauty of God's being is evident. In Edwards' doctrine of the Trinity, his ontology, theology, and understanding of beauty have their origin and integration. For Edwards, God is a triune society of love and beauty.

Edwards' epistemology, especially as it relates to that of John Locke, is discussed in chapter two. For now, it is important to note that for Edwards, and for Locke as well, an actual idea of something is the very thing again. It is the thing repeated. In miscellany #782, Edwards writes:

> To have an actual idea of a thought is to have that thought, that we have an idea of, then in our minds. To have an actual idea of any pleasure or delight, there must be excited a degree of that delight; so to have an actual idea of any trouble or kind of pain, there must be executed a degree of that pain or trouble; and to have an idea of any affection of the mind, there must be then present a degree of that affection.[44]

In a similar vein, Edwards records this entry in "The Mind": "Ideas, all sorts of ideas of things are but the repetitions of those very things over again, as well the ideas of colors, figures, solidity, tastes and smells, as the ideas of thought and mental acts."[45]

Edwards applies this epistemological concept to his doctrine of the Trinity. In miscellany #238, entitled "Trinity," Edwards states this principle of repetition, then relates it to God's being:

> But if the idea be perfect, it is only the same thing absolutely over again. Now if that be certain, as it seems to me to be, then it's quite clear that if God doth think of himself and understand himself with perfect clearness fullness and distinctness, that that idea he hath of himself is absolutely himself again, and is God perfectly to all intents and purposes.

---

[43] Miscellany, #117, Yale 13, p. 284; also in Harvey G. Townsend, ed. *The Philosophy of Jonathan Edwards From His Private Notebooks* (Eugene: University of Oregon, 1955; reprint, Westport: Greenwood Press, 1972), p. 258 (page citations are to the reprint edition).
[44] Miscellany, #782, Townsend, p. 115. For a fuller discussion of this important miscellany, see chapter 2.
[45] "The Mind," #66, Yale 6, p. 383.

That [idea] which God hath of the divine nature and essence is really and fully the divine nature and essence again; so that by God's thinking of himself the Deity must certainly be generated.[46]

God has an actual idea of Himself. That idea is so perfect (indeed, according to Edwards, all of God's ideas are perfect actual ideas) that it is a clear and concise repetition of Himself. God's perfect idea of Himself is God again in the person of God's Son. In other words God the Son is the perfect idea that God the Father has of Himself: "And this person is the second person of the Trinity, the only begotten and dearly beloved Son of God; He is the eternal, necessary, perfect, substantial and personal idea which God hath of Himself."[47]

Here, in God's having an idea of Himself, there is relatedness within God's being. However, in order for God to be the foundation of being and beauty—that is, for God to be excellent—there must be consent as well. For Edwards, the Holy Spirit is that consent. The Holy Spirit is God's infinite and eternal love of and consent to the idea of Himself: "The Holy Spirit is the act of God between the Father and the Son infinitely loving and delighting in each other. Sure I am, that if the Father and the Son do infinitely delight in each other, there must be an infinitely pure and perfect act between them, an infinitely sweet energy we call delight."[48] The Holy Spirit is God's infinite consent to being. The Holy Spirit is God's inner-trinitarian love, God's beauty.

This brings us to a significant juncture as we consider Edwards and beauty. For Edwards, *God's Holy Spirit is Beauty*. For Edwards, beauty is not so much a thing or an idea as it is a divine person in relation. Beauty has a personal identity. All other beauties of proportion, consent, or love find their source in God's beauty. All beauties are derived from and point to God, who, in very being, specifically in the person of the Holy Spirit, is proportion, consent, love, and beauty.

Beauty and Glory

Several important concepts are related to Edwards' understanding of God as a triune society of love and beauty. For example, Edwards ends the first entry of "The Mind" by stating that happiness consists in the perception of being's

---

[46] Miscellany, #238, Yale 13, p. 354; also in Townsend, pp. 247, 248.
[47] "An Essay on the Trinity" in Paul Helm ed. *Treatise on Grace and Other Posthumously Published Writings* (Greenwood: Attic Press, 1971), p. 103.
[48] Miscellany, #94, Yale 13, p. 260.

consent to being. The Trinity is an infinite society of being infinitely consenting to being. Thus God is infinitely happy. Edwards can speak of this happiness, this infinite consent to being, as God's fullness: "there is an infinite fullness of all possible good in God, a fullness of every perfection, of all excellency and beauty, and of infinite happiness."[49]

It is out of God's fullness, as a society of infinite beauty, consent, and happiness, that God was moved to create the world. Creation is the overflow of God's beauty: "Therefore to speak more strictly according to truth, we may suppose that a disposition in God, as an original property of his nature, to an emanation of his own infinite fullness, was what excited him to create the world; and so the emanation itself was aimed at by him as a last end of the creation."[50]

Here it is important to introduce another term related to beauty and excellency: *glory*. For Edwards, glory functions on two important levels. God's glory is God's excellency, beauty, and fullness within the triune society of the Godhead. But glory also stands for the overflow of God's excellency or beauty into creation. The term glory can be used "to express the exhibition, emanation or communication of the internal glory."[51]

Several implications follow. First, all of creation is the result of the overflow of God's fullness and beauty. Now it can be more clearly understood, as noted above, that for Edwards, the structure of being is beauty. Being is proportion. The natural world exemplifies certain laws of proportionality. Natural beauty points beyond itself to spiritual beauty. It does so because the natural world is the product of God's beauty.

Second, it is intelligent being that is properly the recipient of this creative overflow. God created the world for the purpose of communicating God's glory and beauty. It is only intelligent being that is capable of receiving and actively consenting to that beauty:

> In the creature's knowing, esteeming, loving, rejoicing in, and praising God, the glory of God is both exhibited and acknowledged; his fullness is received and returned. Here is both an emanation and remanation. The refulgence shines upon and into the creature, and is reflected back to the luminary. The beams of glory come from God, and are something of God, and are refunded back again to the original. So that the whole is of God, and in God, and to God; and God is the beginning, middle and end in the affair.[52]

---

[49] *Dissertation Concerning the End For Which God Created the World* in Yale 8, pp. 432, 433. For happiness as being's consent to being, see "The Mind," #1, Yale 6, p. 338.
[50] *Dissertation Concerning the End*, Yale 8, p. 435.
[51] Ibid., pp. 513 and 515.
[52] Ibid., p. 531.

Third, this creative overflow of God's glory, in a manner of speaking, enlarges God's being and being in general:

> The first Being, the eternal and infinite Being, is in effect, Being in general; and comprehends universal existence . . . God in his benevolence to his creatures, can't have his heart enlarged in such a manner as to take in being that he finds, who are originally out of himself, distinct and independent. This can't be in an infinite being, who exists alone from eternity. But he, from his goodness, as it were enlarges himself in a more excellent and divine manner. This is by communicating and diffusing himself; and so instead of finding, making objects of his benevolence; not by taking into himself what he finds distinct from himself, and so partaking of their good, and being happy in them; but by flowing forth, and expressing himself in them, and making them to partake of him, and rejoicing in himself expressed in them, and communicated to them.[53]

As God is, as it were, enlarged through the overflow of internal glory and beauty, the perception of God's beauty enlarges the perceiving being. It is being consenting to Being in general.[54]

Fourth, it is the Holy Spirit, as God's beauty, who is the agent of this communication:

> It was more especially the Holy Spirit's work to bring the world to its beauty and perfection out of the chaos, for the beauty of the world is a communication of God's beauty. The Holy Spirit is the harmony and excellency and beauty of the Deity, as we have shown; therefore, 'twas his work to communicate beauty and harmony to the world, and so we read that it was he that moved upon the face of the waters.[55]

Or as he states in another place, "Hence we learn that God's fulness does consist in the Holy Spirit."[56]

Fifth, this overflow of God's beauty and glory is an actual communication from God to the creature. The creature actually experiences the communication of God's beauty through the Holy Spirit. The Holy Spirit is both the agent and the content of this communication:

---

[53] Ibid., pp. 461, 462. See also Ramsey's appendix iii, "Heaven is a Progressive State," pp. 706–738.

[54] R. R. Niebuhr writes that "Edwards' mystical empiricism or empirical mysticism expresses the vocation of human beings to add to the excellency of the created world." Or, as Niebuhr states; for Edwards, "To apprehend with the divine energy of spiritual consent to or love of that which is excellent is to take part in the enlargement of being in general and so in the enlargement of the divine life itself." See *Streams of Grace*, pp. 33 and 35.

[55] Miscellany, #293, Yale 13, p. 384.

[56] "Treatise on Grace" in Helm, p. 65.

the emanation or communication of the divine fullness . . . has relation indeed both to God and the creature; but it has relation to God as its fountain, as it is an emanation from God; and as the communication itself or thing communicated, is something divine, something of God, something of his internal fullness; as the water in the stream is something of the fountain; and as the beams are of the sun.[57]

It is important to note that for Edwards, genuine religious experience involves a reception of God's beauty, through a communication or, as we shall see, an actual infusion of God's Holy Spirit in the saint:

God's Spirit or His love doth but, as it were come and dwell in our hearts and act there as a vital principle, as we become the living temples of the Holy Ghost, and when men are regenerated and sanctified, God pours forth of His Spirit upon them and they have fellowship, or which is the same thing, are made partakers with the Father and Son of their love, i.e., of their joy and beauty.[58]

Last, it is the saints, those who have experienced God's beauty through the sense of the heart, who are the most proper focus and receptacles for God's external glory, beauty, and happiness. Edwards writes that "God has a real delight in the spiritual loveliness of the saints, whose delight is not a delight distinct from what He has in Himself, but is to be resolved into the delight He has in Himself."[59] Krister Sairsingh states that for Edwards, "the church is the community which re-presents the divine community of consent. And in this human community of co-consenters to being in general, the divine glory becomes visible."[60] Or as Sang Lee says, the church for Edwards is the world as it was intended to be.[61]

---

[57] *Dissertation Concerning the End*, Yale 8, p. 531.
[58] "An Essay on the Trinity" in Helm, p. 111.
[59] Miscellany, #79, Townsend, p. 138.
[60] Krister Sairsingh, "Jonathan Edwards and the Idea of Divine Glory: His Foundational Trinitarianism and its Ecclesial Import" (Ph.D. diss., Harvard University, Cambridge, 1986), p. 287.
[61] Lee, *Philosophical Theology*, p. 22.

II

The Experience of Beauty

In his classic analysis of the psychology of religious experience entitled *Religious Affections*, Edwards wrote,

> There is no question whatsoever, that is of greater importance to mankind, and that it more concerns every individual person to be well resolved in, than this, what are the distinguishing qualifications of those that are in favor with God, and entitled to his eternal rewards? Or, which comes to the same thing, What is the nature of true religion?[62]

Although, according to John E. Smith, Edwards never used the phrase "religious experience," he was indeed interested in analyzing and understanding the "nature of true religion." To Edwards, true religion was a work of God's Spirit in a person's life, especially a person or persons who were affected by the religious revivals which he so thoroughly chronicled. Edwards wanted to distinguish "experimental religion," "experiential religion," or "heart religion" (terms which, according to Smith, may be used synonymously) from what was not such "genuine" or "true" religious experience.[63] What did Edwards mean by genuine religious experience? Of particular importance is Edwards' idea of the sense of the heart: Edwards understood the sense of the heart as, among other things, an experience of beauty. Further, this experience of beauty is at the center of Edwards' understanding of the nature of genuine

---

[62] *Religious Affections*, Yale 2, p. 84.

[63] John E. Smith, *Jonathan Edwards, Puritan, Preacher and Philosopher* (Notre Dame: University of Notre Dame Press, 1992), p. 56 note 5. Smith says that the phrase "religious experience" was made popular by William James in his 1902 study *The Varieties of Religious Experience*. Edwards does, however, use the phrase "Christian experience" in *Religious Affections*. See, for example, Yale 2, p. 452. Throughout this present study, the phrase "religious experience" means the range of designations by which Edwards referred to genuine, gracious, experiential, experimental, true, Christian, heart religion.

religious experience. For Edwards, beauty is the very structure of religious experience.

A Sense of the Heart

It has been called Edwards' most distinctive and creative theological contribution: "No idea in all of Edwards' works is more original and no doctrine was more far reaching in its influence upon the course of Puritan piety." John E. Smith penned those words in his introduction to the Yale series publication of Edwards' *Religious Affections*. The doctrine Smith described was that of the "new sense," or what Edwards termed the "sense of the heart."[64] The sense of the heart is understood by interpreters of Edwards in a variety of ways. For Smith, the sense of the heart is seen as the channel through which people lay hold of God. It is a sense through which God's glory is apprehended. Smith says, "This sense is *not* one of the five 'natural' senses; it is a *new creation*, given only to those regenerated by the Spirit."[65] Smith notes that for Edwards, this new sense was "a taste of the beauty of the divine gloria."[66] Sang Lee agrees that the sense of the heart is not a new natural sense or a separate faculty. For Lee, Edwards' sense of the heart is an aesthetic sense and a new disposition or habit of the mind's ordering or knowing. It is "an active tendency of the entire self that determines the direction of all the functions of the human self."[67] Norman Fiering likens the sense of the heart to the kind of "intellectual illumination" described by Francis Hutcheson, a taste that enables one to perceive spiritual beauty. Fiering makes it clear that Edwards' idea of the sense of the heart is very broad in range and complex in meaning. Indeed, Fiering states, "In the face of such an ambiguous and multifaceted concept, it is legitimate to ask: Does this complex have a center out of which

---

[64] John E. Smith in *Religious Affections*, Yale 2, p. 3. James Hoopes correctly points out that interpreters of Edwards have not always clearly differentiated between Edwards' idea of the "new sense" or the "new spiritual sense" and the idea of the "sense of the heart." As Hoopes notes and as we shall see, the "sense of the heart" is, for Edwards, "a broad category that includes various experiences of both saints and sinners." However, the "new spiritual sense" is experienced only by the saints. See James Hoopes, "Jonathan Edwards's Religious Psychology," *Journal of American History* (69) 1983, pp. 857 and 858. In our study the phrases "sense of the heart," "new sense," and "spiritual sense," as they relate to genuine religious experience, are taken as synonymous.

[65] Smith in *Religious Affections*, Yale 2, p. 30. In *Religious Affections*, Edwards makes it quite clear that the sense of the heart is not to be understood as a new faculty of the mind. He writes, "This new spiritual sense, and the new dispositions that attend it, are no new faculties, but are new principles of nature." See *Religious Affections*, Yale 2, p. 206.

[66] Smith in *Religious Affections*, Yale 2, p. 30. Smith is not the only interpreter to link the sense of the heart with Edwards' idea of beauty. See, for example, Delattre, *Beauty and Sensibility*.

[67] Lee, *Philosophical Theology*, p. 150.

its properties radiate?"⁶⁸ It is my contention that there is such a center. It is Edwards' idea of beauty that provides the center for understanding the sense of the heart, especially as that concept is related to Edwards' psychology of religious experience.

Terrence Erdt argues that for Edwards, the sense of the heart was an aesthetic experience of *suavitas* or sweetness. Erdt states that such an experience had long been a part of the Puritan Calvinist tradition: "The sense of the heart was fundamental in Calvinism, indeed it designated the religious experience itself."⁶⁹ This sense of *suavitas* is seen by Erdt to be an essential component in John Calvin's theology and in Calvinistic Puritanism. Edwards' unique contribution to that tradition "was to define, apparently as a result of his own experimental knowledge of regeneration, suavitas as an aesthetic response and to do so as far as possible in Lockean terms."⁷⁰ Erdt renders useful service in stressing the importance of the Calvinistic heritage implicit in Edwards' idea of the sense of the heart. Further, he rightly identifies the sense of the heart as an aesthetic experience. In Edwards' idea of the sense of the heart, one can see a merger of important strains in Edwards' theological and philosophical heritage. Edwards was indeed a Calvinist. Perry Miller argues that he was America's first real Calvinist. But he was also a student of Enlightenment philosophy, borrowing and adapting ideas from a wide range of thinkers including the Cambridge Platonists, the Earle of Shaftsbury, Francis Hutcheson, Niclos Malebranche, and John Locke.⁷¹ In addition, it should be noted that for Edwards, the sense of the heart was more than an experience of *suavitas*; it was more than an aesthetic feeling. For Edwards, the sense of the heart, as it was related to religious experience, was an actual experience of beauty. Erdt is right, however, in that Edwards was describing his own religious experience and religious experience in general in predominantly Lockean terms.

---

⁶⁸ Norman Fiering, *Jonathan Edwards's Moral Thought and Its British Context* (Chapel Hill: University of North Carolina Press, 1981), p. 123.

⁶⁹ Terrence Erdt, *Jonathan Edwards, Art and the Sense of the Heart* (Amherst: University of Massachusetts Press, 1980), p. 20.

⁷⁰ Ibid., p. 23. Erdt cites Calvin's *Institutes of the Christian Religion* in several places. For example, on p. 12 he quotes from III.ii.41 where Calvin states: "But how can the mind be aroused to taste the divine goodness without at the same time being wholly kindled to love God in return? For truly, that abundant sweetness [*suavitatis affluentia*] which God has stored up for those who fear him cannot be known without at the same time powerfully moving us." He also cites III.ii.15 where Calvin says that a feeling of full assurance of salvation "cannot happen without our truly feeling its sweetness and experiencing it in ourselves." See p. 14.

⁷¹ Perry Miller's extravagant statement that Edwards was America's first real Calvinist is found in his essay "The Marrow of Puritan Divinity" in *Errand into the Wilderness* (Cambridge: Harvard University Press, 1956), p. 98. On Edwards and the Enlightenment, see Henry F. May, *The Enlightenment in America* (New York: Oxford University Press, 1976).

Therefore, a key to understanding what Edwards meant by the sense of the heart is to understand its place in his appropriation of Lockean epistemology.

Religious Knowledge

In 1948, one year before his monumental biography of Edwards, Perry Miller published a ground-breaking article in the *Harvard Theological Review*. That article was entitled, "Jonathan Edwards on the Sense of the Heart." After a brief introduction, Miller transcribed an, until then, obscure miscellany, numbered 782, entitled "Ideas, Sense Of The Heart, Spiritual Knowledge Or Conviction. Faith." In that miscellany, Edwards delineated the epistemological foundation of his understanding of knowledge in general and religious knowledge in particular. It was here in Edwards' musings on the nature of knowledge that Miller saw Edwards' appropriation of elements in the epistemology of John Locke.[72]

Edwards begins the miscellany by observing that people often make use of signs in place of ideas: "Great part of our thoughts and the discourse of our minds concerning [things] is without the actual ideas of those things of which we discourse and reason; but the mind makes use of signs instead of the ideas themselves."[73] Edwards notes that when reading a page from a book, a person mentally encounters many signs that properly signify ideas. However, it is impossible to have in the mind the actual ideas that the words signify. So the mind habitually substitutes signs in the place of those ideas. Not only words signify ideas, but ideas may function as signs in the place of other more complex ideas.

For Edwards, sensations may also serve as signs, especially as they relate to particular ideas. This will prove to be an important point, for, as we shall see, in Edwards' religious psychology, especially as it is developed in his treatise on *Religious Affections*, certain religious sensations or "affections" may function as signs of the presence of the Holy Spirit and thus of genuine religious experience. In that treatise, it is clearly the semiotic nature of religious affections, not that of language or ideas, that is of interest to Edwards.[74]

In miscellany #782, Edwards then makes an important affirmation regarding the nature of the mind's ideas:

---

[72] Perry Miller, "Jonathan Edwards on the Sense of the Heart," *Harvard Theological Review* 41 (1948). Wallace E. Anderson in his introduction to Edwards' *Scientific and Philosophical Writings* (Yale 6, p. 120), correctly states, "Edwards used Locke's views more as a foil for developing his own conception of the spiritual world than as a source or authority for it."

[73] Miscellany, #782, in Townsend, p. 113. Wilson Kimnach says that Miscellany #782 was "probably written late in the 1730's." See his introduction in Yale 10, p. 200. It appears that a date of late 1738 or 1739 is appropriate.

[74] See my discussion of *Religious Affections* in chapter 4.

> To have an actual idea of a thought is to have that thought, that we have an idea of, then in our minds. To have an actual idea of any pleasure or delight, there must be excited a degree of that delight; so to have an actual idea of any trouble or kind of pain, there must be excited a degree of that pain or trouble; and to have an idea of any affection of the mind, there must be then present a degree of that affection.[75]

The use of signs is necessary because actual ideas of a thing or perception repeat or reproduce the thing or perception in the mind. Edwards makes a similar point in his notebook "The Mind." There he writes, "All sorts of ideas of things are but repetitions of those very things over again, as well as ideas of colors, figures, solidity, tastes and smells, as the ideas of thought and mental acts."[76] Without the use of signs, the mind's activity would be hopelessly bogged down. Referring again to the example of a person reading a page from a book, Edwards continues:

> We are under a necessity of putting signs in our minds instead of the actual ideas of the things signified, on several accounts: partly by reason of the difficulty of exciting the actual ideas of things, especially in things that are not external and sensible, which are a kind of things that we are mainly concerned with; and also because, if we must have actual ideas of everything that comes in our way in the course of our thought, this would render our thoughts so slow as to render our powers of thinking in a great measure useless, as may be seen in the instance mentioned of a man reading down a page.[77]

Thinking by signs does indeed allow the mind to relate to a greater number of ideas and to relate to highly complex ideas. The mind knows "how to use the sign as if it were the idea itself." The mind has learned through repeated experience to "habitually" connect the sign with that which is signified.[78] However, not having the actual ideas in the mind may and indeed does contribute to errors in thinking and "cause mankind to run into a multitude of errors, the falsity of which would be manifest to them if the ideas themselves were present."[79]

---

[75] Miscellany, #782 in Townsend, p. 115. In this miscellany, Edwards is chiefly concerned with ideas that reflection furnishes to us.
[76] See "The Mind," #66 in Yale 6, p. 383. This principle is especially important for Edwards' idea of the Trinity; see Miscellany, #238 in Yale 13, p. 354.
[77] Miscellany, #782 in Townsend p. 117. According to Edwards, God does not need to utilize signs because all of God's ideas are actual ideas.
[78] Miscellany, #782 in Townsend, p. 117.
[79] Ibid., p. 118. For Edwards, signs are never perfect substitutes for the real thing or idea. This will be an important point for my discussion on the signs of gracious religious experience.

Thinking only by signs Edwards calls "mere cogitation." It is "a kind of mental reading," apprehending things or ideas only indirectly through their signs. In contrast, there is a thinking by "actual ideas." Edwards calls such thinking "apprehension" or having a "direct ideal view or comprehension of the thing thought of." Such knowing he sometimes labels "ideal apprehension." An ideal apprehension can be of things related to the faculty of understanding, "figuratively called the head." This includes "the modes of mere discerning, judging, or speculation." Or the apprehension can be of things related to the faculty of the will, "figuratively called the heart." Heart knowledge includes "all agreeableness and disagreeableness, all beauty and deformity, all pleasure and pain, and all those sensations, exercises, and passions of the mind that arise from either of those." Edwards says that the ideal apprehension associated with the heart is "vulgarly called having a sense."[80]

One of the most important distinctions Edwards makes in this miscellany is the distinction between speculative knowledge and sensible knowledge.[81] For Edwards, knowledge is either speculative, or it is sensible; it is either what he called head knowledge or heart knowledge. Head knowledge pertains to the understanding. Heart knowledge, or sensible knowledge, is experiential: that is, it engages not just a person's understanding, but also his or her will. This kind of sensible knowledge he calls having a sense of the heart.[82] The sense of the heart does not necessarily involve religious knowledge. However, as we shall see, all genuine religious knowledge involves the sense of the heart.

Throughout his writings, Edwards uses honey to illustrate the difference between speculative and sensible knowledge. A person may know that honey is sweet by reading of its flavor in a book or by being told of its sweetness by another person. This kind of knowledge is real knowledge. The person does indeed know that honey is sweet. However, that knowledge is limited and altogether different from the knowledge derived from tasting honey for oneself: "There is a difference between having a rational judgment that honey is sweet, and having a sense of its sweetness. A man may have the former that knows not how honey tastes; but a man cannot have the latter unless he has an

---

[80] Miscellany, #782 in Townsend, p. 119.

[81] In the idea of "sensation" or "sensible knowledge," Edwards is utilizing terminology similar to that of John Locke. For Locke, the mind is a "white page," devoid of innate ideas. Ideas must be provided through the senses or by the mind's reflection upon what is received through the senses. See Locke, *An Essay Concerning Human Understanding*, ed. Peter H. Nidditch (Oxford: Clarendon Press, 1975) bk. 2, ch. 1, secs. 1–4. James Hoopes has convincingly demonstrated that although Edwards utilizes the Lockean language of sensation, his concerns are very different from those of Locke, especially related to Locke's "materialism." See Hoopes, "Jonathan Edwards's Religious Psychology," pp. 849–85, esp. pp. 850 and 851.

[82] Miscellany, #782 in Townsend, p. 119.

idea of the taste of honey in his mind."[83] The latter knowledge is sensible knowledge, derived through the sense of taste. The sweetness is known through experience. Something of the sweetness is actually imparted to the knower.

Although in describing sensible knowledge Edwards often uses positive imagery like that of the sweetness of honey, the sense of the heart can involve sensible knowledge of both positive and negative things:

> all ideal apprehension of beauty and deformity, or loveliness and hatefulness; and all ideas of delight or comfort, or pleasure of body or mind, pain, trouble, or misery; and all ideal apprehensions of desires and longings, esteem, acquiescence, hope, fear, contempt, choosing, refusing, assenting, rejecting, loving, hating, anger, and the idea of all the affections of the mind, and all their motions and exercises; and all ideal views of dignity or excellency of any kind; and also all ideas of terrible greatness, or awful majesty, meanness, or contemptibleness, value and importance. All knowledge of this sort, as it is of things that concern the heart or the will and affections, so it all relates to good or evil that the sensible knowledge of things of this nature involves. And nothing is called a sensible knowledge upon any other account but on the account of the sense or kind of inward tasting or feeling of sweetness or pleasure, bitterness or pains, that is implied in it or arises from it.[84]

It is also possible for positive and negative sensations to coalesce in a sensible knowledge of a singular idea. This is the case in a sense of the heart related to beauty. A sense of beauty may involve a conjunction of diverse, even antithetical sensations, or proportions and disproportions, pleasure and displeasure—a point that will be significant in considering the sense of the heart related to religious experience as an experience of beauty.

What is important here is that for Edwards, there are different kinds or levels of sensible knowledge. The first kind Edwards calls "purely natural." The other kinds involve degrees of the operation of the Holy Spirit. The knowledge of the sweetness of the taste of honey, for example, is "purely natural" sensible knowledge. Natural sensible knowledge is "such as men's minds come to be impressed with, by objects that are about them, by laws of nature; or when they behold anything that is beautiful or deformed, by a beauty or deformity that men by nature are sensible of."[85] "Natural men," says Edwards, "have very little sensible knowledge of the things of religion."[86]

---

[83] "Divine and Supernatural Light" in *The Works of Jonathan Edwards*, vol. 1, Edward Hickman, ed., 2 vols., first published in 1834 (Edinburgh: Banner of the Truth Trust, 1974), p. 14. See also *Religious Affections*, Yale 2, p. 20.
[84] Miscellany, #782 in Townsend, pp. 119 and 120.
[85] Ibid., 121.
[86] Ibid., 123.

There is another kind of natural sensible knowledge that is not "purely natural." After making the important distinction between speculative and sensible knowledge, Edwards applies that distinction to the epistemology of religious experience. People, unaided by grace, are capable of having a measure of speculative and sensible knowledge of God and matters of religion. They may know content or information about God and religion. When a person, however, through the preaching of the Word, comes under conviction or awakening, the Holy Spirit, says Edwards, assists or heightens that natural knowledge. Thus the spiritually awakened person is made to sense, to feel, or in a certain manner to experience the reality of God, or of hell, or of other spiritual things, in a more vivid way. This is why painting such graphic word pictures of spiritual truths was so important to Edwards. Such preaching aided by the Holy Spirit helped natural religious knowledge become more sensible religious knowledge. In preaching about hell, for example, Edwards labored to give his hearers a sense or feeling of the reality of hell as he understood it.[87] However, this sensible knowledge, although aided by the Holy Spirit, is still a natural sensibility:

> Natural men, while they are senseless and unawakened, have very little sensible knowledge of the things of religion . . . But when they are awakened and convinced, the Spirit of God, by assisting their natural powers, gives 'em an ideal apprehension of the things of religion with respect to what is natural in them, i.e., of that which is speculative in them, and that which pertains to a sensibleness of their natural good or evil . . . In thus assisting men's faculties to an ideal apprehension of the natural things of religion, together with what assistance God may give men's natural reason and judgment to see the force of natural arguments, consists the whole of the common work of the Spirit of God in man. It consists only in assisting natural principles *without infusing anything supernatural*.[88]

This assisting function is part of the common or ordinary work of the Holy Spirit. There is nothing "supernatural" in it; rather, it consists "in giving a sense of the spiritual and eternal things, or things that appertain to the business of religion and our eternal interest." Edwards is careful to note that there is no new revelatory content in such Spirit-assisted knowledge. He does

---

[87] On preaching about hell, see Fiering's chapter entitled "Hell and the Humanitarians" in *Jonathan Edwards's Moral Thought*, pp. 200–260. Fiering makes the point that Edwards' preaching on hell was extraordinary only in its rhetorical power, not in its content. For an excellent discussion of Edwards' preaching theory and practice related to sensibility, see Wilson Kimnach's introduction in Yale 10, pp. 199–207.

[88] Miscellany, #782 in Townsend, pp. 123 and 124. Emphasis added.

not want to encourage "enthusiasm." Indeed, he says, "the ordinary influence of God's Spirit communicates only a sensible knowledge of those things that the mind had a speculative knowledge of before."[89] This natural sensible religious knowledge, Edwards says, "we commonly call conviction." Conviction consists in an ideal view of God's greatness manifested in creation and in scripture. Under conviction, people are assisted to "a sensible apprehension of the heinousness of sin" and God's wrath in response to sin. They are made sensible of the importance of religion and the necessity for salvation.[90] Such sensible knowledge is not salvific; however, it is part of the process of preparation toward saving faith.[91] Saving conviction cannot be attained merely by the Spirit's assisting activity; rather, knowledge that is salvific may be derived only by "the immediate influence of the Spirit of God on men's hearts."[92]

There is a "spiritual" sensible knowledge that is derived beyond natural human abilities of knowing. This knowledge is supernatural, in that the Holy Spirit does more than assist natural capacities. This is knowledge available only to the saints; indeed, sainthood is defined in part by this knowledge. There is a "difference between the influence of the Spirit of God on the minds of natural men in awakenings, common convictions, and illuminations, and His spiritual influences on the hearts of the saints at and after their conversion."[93] Edwards continues:

> The spiritual work of the Spirit of God, or that which is peculiar to the saints, consists in giving the sensible knowledge of the things of religion with respect to their spiritual good or evil, which indeed does all originally consist in a sense of the spiritual excellency, beauty, or sweetness of divine things. This is not by assisting natural principles but by infusing something supernatural.[94]

Something supernatural is infused into the soul. The content of that supernatural infusion is relevant: for Edwards, it is God's very Spirit that is infused into the saint. But it is important to note the kind of knowledge derived through such an infusion:

---

[89] Miscellany, #782 in Townsend, p. 122. There is an "extraordinary" influence of the Holy Spirit which Edwards calls "inspiration." Here the Spirit is said to impart "speculative knowledge to the soul" (p. 122).

[90] Miscellany, #782 in Townsend, p. 123.

[91] On Edwards' doctrine of preparation, see John H. Gerstner, *Steps to Salvation: The Evangelistic Message of Jonathan Edwards* (Philadelphia: Westminster Press, 1960).

[92] Miscellany, #782 in Townsend, p. 124.

[93] Ibid., p. 123.

[94] Ibid., p. 124.

> An ideal and sensible apprehension of the spiritual excellency of divine things is [the] proper source of all spiritual conviction of the truth of divine things, or that belief of their truth that is in saving faith. There can be no saving conviction without it, and it is the great thing that mainly distinguishes saving belief from all other. And the thing wherein its distinguishing essence does properly lie [is] that it has a sense of the divine spiritual excellency of the things of religion as that which it arises from. All saving conviction of divine truth does most effectively arise from the spiritual sense of the excellency of divine things.[95]

This supernatural, spiritual, sensible knowledge is the constitutive element of the conviction that eventuates in saving faith. Its content is the excellency or beauty of divine things. It is this sensible knowledge of divine excellency that is distinctive of efficacious religious experience.

There is an interplay between the sensible knowledge of religion and divine things acquired through the Spirit's assistance of natural capacities and the sensible knowledge that is supernatural and spiritual; indeed the latter knowledge is predicated upon the former knowledge. There is, says Edwards, a "congruity," a "perfect fitness" or "perfect suitableness" between the two.[96]

It is in the interplay and interdependence of the knowledge that is Spirit-assisted natural knowledge and the knowledge that is supernatural, spiritual, Spirit-infused knowledge that we see an important principle related to Edwards' idea of beauty. The religious knowledge associated with the sense of the heart may involve a conjunction of religious sensations in one religious experience. There is certainly a relatedness between natural and supernatural knowledge. Further, this relatedness may bring together sensations which, taken on their own, may appear antithetical and mutually exclusive. A sense of the excellency or beauty of God's glory, God's grace and mercy, and the beauty of the way of salvation through Christ is accompanied with and related to a sense of one's unworthiness, one's guilt and misery as a sinner, and the justness of one's condemnation. These sensations are conjoined to form one religious experience. In Edwards' language of beauty, such an experience would be intensely and complexly beautiful.[97]

Before ending the miscellany, Edwards makes one other important observation related to Spirit-assisted versus Spirit-infused knowledge. People under conviction see the agreeableness, the suitableness, or the fitness or congruity

---

[95] Ibid., p. 125.

[96] Ibid., p. 126. On the idea of "fitness" in Edwards, see Wilson Kimnach's discussion in Yale 10, p. 203. Kimnach points out that although there is not a causal link between sensible preaching—that is, preaching for sensible effect—and conversion, there is, nevertheless, for Edwards a "fitness" between the two.

[97] Miscellany, #782 in Townsend, p. 125.

between the seemingly disparate sensations. Common conviction contributes to saving conviction in that:

> [M]en, by being made sensible of the great guilt of sin or the connection or natural agreeableness there is between that and a dreadful punishment, and how that the greatness and majesty of God seems to require and demand such a punishment, they are brought to see the great need of a satisfaction or something to intervene to make it honorable to that majesty to show 'em favor; and being for a while blind to the suitableness of Christ's satisfaction in order to this, and then afterwards having a sense given them of Christ's divine excellency and so of the glorious dignity of His person and what He did and suffered for sinners, hereby their eyes are, as it were, opened to see the perfect fitness there is in this to satisfy for sin and to render their being received into favor consistent with the honor of God's offended majesty. The sight of this excellent congruity does very powerfully convince of the truth of the Gospel.[98]

One might say that for Edwards they see and experience the beauty of it.[99] Indeed, it is this experiential or sensible knowledge of beauty that enables one to cross the epistemological gap from being an awakened, convicted sinner to being a converted saint.

A Sense of the Spirit

The exposition of Edwards' miscellany #782 gives us important foundational principles for understanding what he means by the sense of the heart and genuine religious experience. These principles can be expanded and applied from his other writings. It is important to understand the content of the Spirit-infused knowledge and the effects and affects of that knowledge in the life of the saint. It is also important to note that that which is actually infused into the life of a person is God's Holy Spirit. The Holy Spirit, who in the vocabulary of Edwards' language of beauty is God's beauty, is actually communicated to the person, infused within him or her:

> The Spirit of God is given to the true saints to dwell in them, as his lasting abode; and to influence their hearts, as a principle of new nature, or as a divine supernatural spring of life and action. The Scriptures represent the Holy Spirit, not only as moving, and occasionally influencing

---

[98] Ibid., pp. 125 and 126.
[99] Wilson Kimnach compares the artistry of Edwards in conveying such knowledge of the beauty of divine things through preaching to the artistry of a sculptor in communicating beauty through art. Both artist and preacher are attempting to effect not just knowledge about beauty, but an actual experience of beauty. See Kimnach's editor's introduction in Yale 10, pp. 203 and 204.

the saints, but as dwelling in them . . . And he is represented as being there so united to the faculties of the soul, that he becomes there a principle or spring of new nature and life.[100]

The sense of the heart, related to genuine religious experience, is thus primarily an experience, an infusion, of God's very being and beauty. The saint becomes a partaker of God's beauty and, in a sense, God's being:

> The [saints] have spiritual excellency and joy by a kind of participation of God. They are made excellent by a communication of God's excellency. God puts his own beauty, i.e., his beautiful likeness upon their souls . . . The saints are beautiful and blessed by a communication of God's holiness and joy . . . the saints have both their spiritual excellency and blessedness by the gift of the Holy Ghost, and his dwelling in them. They are not only caused by the Holy Ghost, but are in him as their principle. The Holy Spirit becoming an inhabitant, is a vital principle in the soul.[101]

For Edwards, the sense of the heart is not only a vehicle or channel of apprehension or perception, it is an actual experience of God.

Edwards tries to avoid the position that God's essence is actually communicated to the saints. He writes, "Not that the saints are made partakers of the essence of God, and are 'Godded' with God, and 'Christed' with Christ, according to the abominable and blasphemous language and notions of some heretics: but to use the Scripture phrase, they are made partakers of God's fullness . . . that is, of God's spiritual beauty and happiness, according to the measure and capacity of a creature."[102] For our purposes it is important to note that the experience of the sense of the heart does involve some type of communication of God to the saints.

The sense of the heart ultimately is the infusion of the Holy Spirit or an actual experience of God's beauty. The new sense is, as Richard R. Niebuhr states, "the gift of the presence of the Holy Spirit."[103] The sense of the heart is thus an actual experience and appropriation of what Edwards describes as beauty itself. This experience is accompanied by a sensible feeling of *suavitas*, a new mode of perception, a new habit or disposition of ordering, and especially a new taste or relish of spiritual beauty. It includes many of the characteristics by which it has been said to be defined. But fundamentally the sense of the heart, as a discriminating factor of genuine religious experience, is best understood as an actual infusion of the one who by definition is beauty. Thus, by definition, the sense of the heart is an aesthetic experience of the deepest kind.

---

[100] *Religious Affections* in Yale 2, p. 200.
[101] "God Glorified in Man's Dependence etc." in Hickman, vol. 2, p. 5.
[102] *Religious Affections* in Yale 2, p. 203.
[103] Niebuhr, *Streams of Grace*, p. 34.

Beauty Perceived

The experience of the sense of the heart dramatically affects one's aesthetic sensibility. A person acquires a new, heightened perception of beauty. The new sense produces a new vision of the beauty of God, of Christ, of divine things in general, and of the portrayal of divine beauty in nature. In his *Treatise on Grace*, Edwards writes that "the first effect of the power of God in the heart in REGENERATION, is to give the heart a Divine taste or sense; to cause it to have a relish of the loveliness and sweetness of the supreme excellency of the Divine nature."[104] Through the regenerating experience of the sense of the heart, saints, made such by that experience, gain a new vision of divine beauty. Indeed, such a new perception is an important first phase in sainthood, directly related to subsequent effects.

Divine beauty may also be perceived in what God has created. Nature portrays the beauty of God. For Edwards the structure of being in general is that of beauty. Sang Lee notes that Edwards has a "thoroughly aesthetic vision of reality." Or, as Lee says, for Edwards, "beauty is what the structure of being... looks like."[105] Consistent with this aesthetic nature of being, Edwards stresses that there is an aesthetic character in the laws of nature by which God governs His creation:

> So much evidence of the most perfect exactness of proportion, harmony, equity, and beauty in the mechanical laws of nature and other methods of providence, which belong to the course of nature, by which God shows his regard to harmony and fitness and beauty in what He does as governor of the natural world, may strongly argue that He will maintain the most strict and perfect justice in proportion and fitness in what He does as governor of the moral world.[106]

The beauty of the natural world is an emblem of spiritual and divine beauty. In a charming essay entitled "Beauty of the World," Edwards writes:

> The beauty of the world consists wholly of sweet mutual consents, either within itself, or with the Supreme Being. As to the corporeal world, though there are many other sorts of consents, yet the sweetest and most charming beauty of it is its resemblance of spiritual beauties. The reason is that spiritual beauties are infinitely the greatest, and bodies being but the shadows of beings, they must be so much the more charming as they shadow forth spiritual beauties.[107]

---

[104] *Treatise on Grace*, ed. Paul Helm, p. 49.
[105] Lee, *Philosophical Theology*, p. 79.
[106] Miscellany, #1196 in Townsend, p. 184.
[107] "Beauty of the World" in Yale 6, p. 305.

Natural beauties, says Edwards, are "shadows" of spiritual beauty. Natural and physical realities can function as types of spiritual realities, fulfilled in the spiritual antitype."[108] Nature portrays divine beauty. Edwards writes that "to find out the reasons of things in natural philosophy is only to find out the proportion of God's acting."[109] Elsewhere Edwards writes that such a perception of beauty is related to the very purpose of human existence:

> [F]or intelligent beings are created to be the consciousness of the universe, that they may perceive what God is and does. This can be nothing else but to perceive the excellency of what he is and does. Yea, he is nothing but excellency; and all that he does, nothing but excellent.[110]

It is especially the task of the saints to perceive the divine beauty portrayed in creation. To the sanctified imagination all beauty is sacramental. Indeed, says Harold Simonson, "it is this sacramental dimension that is visible only to the sanctified imagination, for there is no sacramental object apart from the special heartfelt sense that grasps it . . . Seen by the regenerate eye, nature is full of divine emanations."[111]

Edwards' concept of the new sense was indeed complex. Although he used the terminology of the sense of the heart to apply to sensible knowledge in general, as distinct from speculative knowledge, the concept was primarily applied to religious knowledge and the distinction between genuine religious experience and religious knowledge that was not salvific. It involved more than a new mode of perception or sense of the mind. It was a sense of the heart, an actual taste or experience of spiritual realities. This sense of the heart was a supernatural infusion of God's Holy Spirit. It was an actual experience of God's being and God's beauty. The accompanying religious sensations were themselves beautiful. Intense sorrow for sin was conjoined with an intense sense of God's glory and excellency. Thus, in the vocabulary of Edwards' language of beauty, the sense of the heart was itself an experience of intense complex beauty.

Related to the sense of the heart, one may say that for Edwards the structure of religious experience was that of beauty. Authentic religious experience began with and was defined by an infusion of the Holy Spirit, God's beauty. Such experience was itself a conjunction of diverse religious sensations. Further, the sense of the heart led to a new awareness and appreciation of beauty.

---

[108] "Images of Divine Things" in Yale 11. See editor's introduction.
[109] "The Mind," #34, Yale 6, p. 353.
[110] Miscellany, #87, Yale 13, p. 252.
[111] Harold P. Simonson, *Jonathan Edwards: Theologian of the Heart* (Grand Rapids, Mich.: Eerdmans, 1974), p. 78.

III

The Manifestation of Beauty

It is a gracious experience of beauty that is at the heart of Edwards' understanding and articulation of genuine religious experience. According to Edwards, sainthood is a work of divine art. The very structure of genuine religious experience is that of beauty. William Clebsch writes that "beauty conveyed the sum of [Edwards'] spirituality: true religion is not to achieve moral goodness but to receive holy beauty."[112] Sang Lee, utilizing Edwards' appropriation of Lockean terminology, says that through the sense of the heart, the saint "becomes, in effect, a 'simple idea' of beauty." Lee further says that "the sense of the heart, therefore, is the aesthetic sensibility of the whole self."[113] To examine the ways in which the vocabulary of Edwards' language of beauty functioned in his theory and descriptions of religious experience through the sense of the heart, one notes the language of beauty in the theory of individual and corporate saintly life. Saints, those who had experienced God's beauty, were to manifest beauty in their lives and affections. Consider the important paradigm of Edwards' Christology.

BEAUTY INCARNATE

For Jonathan Edwards it is in the person and work of Christ that God's beauty is most dramatically and most personally made manifest. For Edwards, Christ is beauty incarnate. Also, Christ is a divine person. Christ, as the second person of the Trinity, is the very idea or repetition of God's being.

---

[112] William A. Clebsch, *American Religious Thought, a History* (Chicago: The University of Chicago Press, 1973), p. 55.
[113] Sang Hyun Lee, "Mental Activity and the Perception of Beauty in Jonathan Edwards" *Harvard Theological Review* 69 (1976), pp. 391 and 389. Also see Lee, *Philosophical Theology*, p. 158. On Edwards' use of the phrase "new simple idea," see *Religious Affections*, Yale 2, p. 205.

The divine beauty of Christ as the second person of the Trinity is manifested through the Incarnation. For Edwards, Christ is the enfleshment of God's beauty. In Edwards' understanding of the Incarnation, several important principles merge. It is God's nature to express Himself *ad intra*, within the Trinity, and *ad extra*, in what God creates.[114] Thus, the beauty of nature is one expression of God's beauty. The beauty of nature is actually an image of the expression of God's beauty revealed in Christ. It is Christ's beauty that is portrayed in and through nature. In a miscellany entitled "Excellency of Christ," Edwards writes that "the beauties of nature are really emanations, or shadows, of the excellencies of the Son of God."[115] Commenting on this passage, Sang Lee observes that for Edwards, "the physical universe also is, in limited degrees, the enfleshment of the beauty of the eternal Son of God."[116] Nature portrays God's beauty expressed in and through Christ. It is, however, Christ's Incarnation itself that is the focal point of God's expression of God's beauty. Through the Incarnation, says Sang Lee, "God's beauty became visible in time and history via the person and work of Jesus of Nazareth and the redemptive history of which Jesus is the center."[117] In regard to Edwards' Christology, Lee also states: "At this point, Edwards' philosophical epistemology and his theological soteriology merge into one doctrine. Objectively, God became incarnate in Jesus Christ, making visible the transcendent beauty of divine being. This manifestation of God's beauty also involved Christ's work of the atonement for human sin."[118] As the second person of the Trinity, Christ manifests God's beauty, the Holy Spirit. This status or condition is not altered by the Incarnation. The incarnate Christ is filled with God's beauty. Roland Delattre writes, "For it is in the Holy Spirit Himself that [Edwards] finds the substantial beauty of God, and the beauty of Christ consists in his being filled with the Spirit." God's beauty is especially made manifest through the divine-human Christ.[119]

An important principle is at work in Edwards' Christology. Briefly stated, this principle is that God's primary beauty will manifest itself in other forms of beauty. God's beauty is evidenced by beauty. Related to Christ, this means

---

[114] For a discussion of Edwards' Trinitarian thought, see chapter 1.
[115] Miscellany, #108 in Yale 13, p. 279.
[116] Lee, *Philosophical Theology*, p. 230.
[117] Ibid., p. 143.
[118] Ibid. James Carse writes: "[Edwards'] Christ is not one we are to think about, his is a Christ we are to see . . . Therefore, one often has the impression that [Edwards] is painting a verbal picture of Christ. The metaphors translate easily into visible components." James Carse, *Jonathan Edwards and the Visibility of God* (New York: Charles Scribner's Sons, 1967), p. 100
[119] Delattre, *Beauty and Sensibility*, p. 157. Delattre also states, "the divine beauty that is the Holy Spirit appears especially in the Son." See p. 156.

that God's primary beauty is made manifest in the incarnate Christ's life and ministry. This principle has important implications for the manifestation of beauty in the life and affections of the saints. For Edwards, when people, through the sense of the heart, have an experience of God's beauty, that experience will be evidenced in other forms of beauty. Edwards describes such an experience using the language of beauty. Further, Edwards portrays the life and affections of the saints, individually and corporately, as those of beauty made manifest. This manifestation of beauty, in both individual saints and saintly society, is the focus of this chapter; it is necessary first, however, to explicate Edwards' graphic portrayal of Jesus Christ as beauty incarnate.

Excellency of Christ

In 1738 Edwards published a group of sermons entitled *Five Discourses on Important Subjects, Nearly Concerning the Great Affair of the Soul's Eternal Salvation*. Four of the five sermons were preached by Edwards in connection with the revivals of 1734 and 1735 which swept through Northampton and the Connecticut River valley. The first discourse, entitled "Justification by Faith Alone," was an expanded version of the sermon to which Edwards credited the beginning of the revivals.[120] The notable exception in the *Five Discourses* was a discourse entitled "The Excellency of Christ." This discourse was not originally preached in connection with the Northampton revivals. In the preface to the *Five Discourses* Edwards wrote that "the following discourses were all, excepting the last, delivered in the time of the late wonderful work of God's power and grace in this place, and are now published in the earnest desire of those to whom they were preached."[121] The last discourse was "The Excellency of Christ." Explaining why he added that sermon for publication Edwards stated:

> What is published at the end, concerning the excellency of Christ, is added on my own motion; thinking that a discourse on such an evangelical subject would properly follow others that were chiefly awakening; and that something of the excellency of the Savior was proper to succeed those things that were to show the necessity of salvation.[122]

---

[120] The text of the *Five Discourses* can be found in Hickman, vol. 1, beginning on p. 620. The discourses include: "Justification by Faith Alone," "Pressing into the Kingdom of God," "Ruth's Resolve," "The Justice of God in the Damnation of Sinners," and "The Excellency of Christ."
[121] "Preface" in Hickman, vol. 1, p. 620.
[122] "Ibid., p. 621. Delattre states that Edwards preached the sermon in 1734. See Delattre, *Beauty and Sensibility*, p. 158.

It seems evident that Edwards viewed the sermon as an important work, one which, although having general applications, was also specifically related to the revivals. Edwards deliberately linked his Christology, especially an understanding of the beauty of Christ, with important discourses on the nature of the religious experiences in the revivals of the 1730's. The sermon "The Excellency of Christ" and the Christology behind it serve as an important paradigm for Edwards' understanding of the nature of religious experience. As early as 1738, I believe, Edwards began directly to relate the concerns of the revivals, especially an understanding of genuine religious experience, to his understanding of beauty.

In this sermon, Edwards demonstrates that the presence of God's primary beauty in the person of the Holy Spirit manifests itself in other forms of beauty. Beauty was made manifest in the one, in this case Christ, who was filled with God's beauty.[123] The very title of the sermon relates Christ in the language of beauty. "Excellency" and "beauty," we have noted, are closely related terms in Edwards' philosophical theology. The title is indeed descriptive of the content of the sermon, in which Edwards paints a beautiful portrait of the beauty of Christ. The text for the sermon is Rev. 5:5, 6, which reads:

> And one of the elders saith unto me, Weep not: behold, the Lion of the tribe of Judah, the Root of David, hath prevailed to open the book, and to loose the seven seals thereof. And I beheld, and, lo, in the midst of the throne and of the four beasts, and in the midst of the elders, stood a Lamb as it had been slain.[124]

The biblical passage from which the text is taken describes an apocalyptic vision experienced by "The Apostle John." In the vision, God, seated on the heavenly throne, is holding a scroll sealed with seven seals. John is weeping because no one can be found who is worthy to break the seals and open the scroll. Then one of the elders attending the throne of God declares that there is indeed one who is worthy. That one of course is Christ. John is told that it is the lion of the tribe of Judah, the root of David who is worthy to open the scroll. In the vision, John turns to look upon the worthy lion but what meets his eyes is not a lion at all; rather what he sees is a lamb, appearing to have been slain. The remainder of the sermon is a thorough exposition of the implications of Christ as both lion and lamb.

It is in the "conjunction" of these two images, that of the lion and the lamb, that Edwards elaborately portrays the beauty and excellency of Christ.

---

[123] See Delattre, *Beauty and Sensibility*, p. 160.

[124] "Excellency of Christ," Hickman, vol. 1, p. 680. The scripture text is quoted from the King James Version.

It should be noted again that in Edwards' understanding, beauty becomes more intensified as more and more disparate entities or characteristics of an entity are harmonized into an integrated whole. Edwards uses such examples as the human body and face to illustrate this point. In both examples a variety of differing sizes and shapes coalesce into a whole entity. The point of the sermon is that the conjunction of various attributes and characteristics in the person and work of Christ, symbolized by the images of the lion and the lamb, render Christ intensely beautiful, infinitely excellent and worthy. Thus the doctrine of the sermon reads, "There is an admirable conjunction of diverse excellencies in Jesus Christ."[125] Edwards continues:

> The lion and the lamb, though very diverse kinds of creatures, yet have each their peculiar excellencies. The lion excels in strength, and in majesty of his appearance and voice: the lamb excels in meekness and patience, besides the excellent nature of the creature as good for food, and yielding that which is fit for our clothing, and being suitable to be offered in sacrifice to God. But we see that Christ is in the text compared to both; because the diverse excellencies of both wonderfully meet in him.[126]

Edwards portrays these conjunctions of excellencies in three stages. In the first stage, he says, "There is a conjunction of such excellencies in Christ, as, in our manner of conceiving, are very diverse one from another." Under this heading Edwards notes that "there do meet in Jesus Christ infinite highness and infinite condescension." Christ's "majesty is infinitely awful;" yet toward sinful, undeserving people, "His condescension is great enough to become their friend; to become their companion, to unite their souls to him in spiritual marriage." Also under this first heading Edwards states that "there meet in Jesus Christ, infinite *justice* and infinite *grace*." Christ is a judge toward sinners; but he is also a gracious savior.[127]

The second heading in which the conjunction of excellencies is shown reads:

> There do meet in the person of Christ such really diverse excellencies, which otherwise would have been thought utterly incompatible in the same subject; such as are conjoined in no other person whatever, either divine, human, or angelical; and such as neither men nor angels would ever have imagined could have met together in the same person, had it not been seen in the person of Christ.[128]

---

[125] "Excellency of Christ," Hickman, vol. 1, p. 680.
[126] Ibid.
[127] Ibid., pp. 680, 681.
[128] Ibid., p. 681.

Here Edwards' rhetorical language is intensified. The conjunctions increase in magnitude. Not even angels could have imagined such conjunctions in the same subject. Thus Christ's beauty is more intensely complex.

The examples given in this section are striking. In Christ there is a merger of infinite *glory* and lowest *humility*, "in Jesus Christ, who is both God and man, those two diverse excellencies are sweetly united." Further, in Christ, infinite *majesty* and transcendent *meekness* are conjoined. Reflecting on the imagery of the text from Revelation, Edwards says: "Thus is Christ a Lion in majesty, and a Lamb in meekness."[129] Edwards offers a number of other examples from Christ's life and work. He states that in Christ there is conjoined

> deepest *reverence* towards God and *equality* with God . . . infinite *worthiness* of good, and the greater *patience* under suffering of evil . . . an exceeding spirit of *obedience*, with supreme *dominion* over heaven and earth; absolute *sovereignty* and perfect *resignation* . . . *self-sufficiency*, and an entire *trust* and reliance on God.[130]

The third heading of this section focuses on the diversity of Christ's excellencies as they are exercised toward people: "Such diverse excellencies are expressed in him towards men, that otherwise would have seemed impossible to be exercised towards the same object."[131] Here, rather briefly in comparison to the other sections, Edwards describes Christ's exercise of justice, mercy, and truth toward men and women.[132]

Thus far Edwards has thoroughly portrayed a diversity of excellencies that are conjoined in the person of Christ. He moves next to describe how an "admirable conjunction of excellencies appears in Christ's acts."[133] He gives a relatively brief overview of Christ's birth and various segments of his life and career:

> This admirable conjunction of excellencies appears in the acts and various passages of Christ's life. Though Christ dwelt in mean outward circumstances, whereby his condescension and humility especially appeared, and his majesty was veiled; yet his divine dignity and glory did in many of his acts shine through the veil, and it illustriously appeared, that he was not only the Son of man, but the great God.[134]

Edwards continues:

---

[129] Ibid., p. 682.
[130] Ibid.
[131] Ibid.
[132] Ibid., pp. 682, 683.
[133] Ibid., p. 683.
[134] Ibid.

Manifestation of Beauty

> At the same time that Christ was wont to appear in such meekness, condescension, and humility, in his familiar discourses with his disciples, appearing therein as the Lamb of God, he was also wont to appear as *the Lion of the tribe of Judah*, with divine authority and majesty, in his so sharply rebuking the scribes and Pharisees, and other hypocrites.[135]

Edwards then focuses on one particular aspect of Christ's work. He is especially interested in portraying the beauty revealed in Christ's death on the cross:

> This admirable conjunction of excellencies remarkably appears in his offering up himself a sacrifice for sinners in his last sufferings. As this was the greatest thing in all the works of redemption, the greatest act of Christ in that work; so in this act especially does there appear that admirable conjunction of excellencies that has been spoken of.[136]

The imagery of the sacrificial lamb is connected with that event. He states: "Christ never so much appeared as a lamb, as when he was slain." However, Edwards also sees Christ's lion-likeness in the cross. He says, "and yet in that act he did in an especial manner appear as '*the Lion of the tribe of Judah*.'"[137]

Edwards elaborates on this theme by listing several examples of a diversity of excellencies coalescing in Christ's death. The cross demonstrates Christ's greatest degree of humiliation, but also his divine glory. In this one act Christ manifested a great love of God; but he also manifested great love of God's enemies. On the cross Christ "never so eminently appeared *for* divine justice, and yet never suffered so much *from* divine justice." Christ's holiness shone forth in the cross; yet he was treated as a guilty sinner. Christ was treated as unworthy, but his vicarious death accounts him as eminently worthy. Edwards continues: "Christ in his last sufferings suffered most extremely from those towards whom he was then manifesting his greatest act of love." And lastly, "It was in Christ's last sufferings, above all, that he was delivered up to the power of his enemies; and yet by these, above all, he obtained victory over his enemies." In a very succinct statement Edwards summarizes Christ's beauty revealed on the cross. On the cross, "Christ appeared at the same time, and in the same act as both a lion and a lamb."[138]

Before moving on to the application section of the sermon, Edwards briefly explores the conjunction of lamblike and lionlike excellencies in Christ in two eschatological categories. First, a conjunction of excellencies

---

[135] Ibid.
[136] Ibid., p. 684.
[137] Ibid.
[138] Ibid., p. 685.

is manifested in Christ's "present state of exaltation in heaven." Secondly, "the admirable conjunction of excellencies will be manifest in Christ's acts at the last judgment." In these events he will be a lion to the reprobate, but a lamb to the saints.[139]

The application section, consistent with the rest of the sermon, is quite remarkable. After having painted a striking portrait of the beauty and excellency of Christ, portrayed in his personal attributes and in his life, death, and glorification, Edwards pleads with his readers to receive and join with such an excellent savior: "Let the consideration of this wonderful meeting of diverse excellencies in Christ induce you to accept of him, and close with him as your Saviour." The beauty of Christ is an inducement to personal awakening and revival:

> And here is not only infinite strength and infinite worthiness, but infinite condescension, and love and mercy, as great as power and dignity. If you are a poor, distressed sinner, whose heart is ready to sink for fear that God never will have mercy on you, you need not be afraid to go to Christ, for fear that he is either unable or unwilling to help you.[140]

The language and pastoral spirit of that section is indeed rich. Beauty, portrayed in the conjunction of diverse excellencies, is *the* characteristic of Christ which renders Christ both attractive and accessible. As Edwards understood the beauty of Christ to be fundamental to Christ's life and work, so too is that beauty important for the experience of Christ's salvific work in the life of the believer. The sermon continues with Edwards raising rhetorical questions aimed at the application of Christ's beauty: "What are you afraid of, that you dare not venture your soul upon Christ? . . . What is there that you can desire should be in a Saviour, that is not in Christ? . . . What excellency is there wanting? . . . What is there wanting, or else would you add if you could, to make him more fit to be your Saviour?"[141]

The final section of the sermon is an improvement of the application:

> Let what has been said be improved to induce you to love the Lord Jesus Christ, and choose him for your friend and portion. As there is such an admirable meeting of diverse excellencies in Christ, so there is everything in him to render him worthy of your love and choice, and to win and engage it. Whatsoever there is or can be desirable in a friend, is in Christ, and that to the highest degree that can be desired.[142]

---

[139] Ibid., p. 686.
[140] Ibid.
[141] Ibid.
[142] Ibid., p. 688.

Manifestation of Beauty

In this final section Edwards introduces the idea of Christ as a friend:

> Would you choose for a friend a person of great dignity? It is a thing taking with men to have those for their friends who are much above them; because they look upon themselves honoured by the friendship of such. Thus, how taking would it be with an inferior maid to be the object of the dear love of some great and excellent prince. But Christ is infinitely above you, and above all the princes of the earth; for he is the King of Kings. So honourable a person as this offers himself to you, in the nearest and dearest friendship.[143]

Christ is not only a *great* friend; He is a *good* friend as well. These two excellencies are also conjoined in Him:

> And could you choose to have a friend not only great but good? In Christ infinite greatness and infinite goodness meet together, and receive luster and glory one from another. His greatness is rendered lovely by his goodness . . . Indeed, goodness is excellent in whatever subject it be found; it is beauty and excellency itself, and renders all excellent that are possessed of it; and yet most excellent when joined with greatness.[144]

After posing a number of rhetorical questions to describe characteristics desirable in a friend, Edwards concludes:

> Thus is Christ. Though he be the great God, yet he has, as it were, brought himself down to be upon a level with you, so as to become man as you are, that he might not only be your Lord, but your brother, and that he might be the more fit to be a companion for such a worm of the dust.[145]

Paul Ramsey states that "Edwards' incarnational Christology is essential to his understanding of Christ as eternally the Mediator of the increase of knowledge, love, and joy in God."[146] Christ as the incarnation of the second person of the Trinity has really been the subject of the entire sermon. It is the union of the divine and human in Christ that has rendered Him eminently excellent, intensely beautiful. Because of the Incarnation of Christ, the mighty God can be a friend and brother to sinners. In closing the sermon, Edwards gives several implications of the incarnation in relation to the experiences of believers.

---

[143] Ibid.
[144] Ibid.
[145] Ibid.
[146] Ramsey in "Appendix III," Yale 8, p. 730.

Having such a beautiful savior for a friend has significant advantages. When one has "closed" with Christ there are tremendous implications for the individual: "by your choosing Christ for your friend and partner, you will obtain these two infinite benefits." The first infinite benefit is that when connected with him, "Christ will give himself to you, with all these various excellencies that meet in him, to your full and everlasting enjoyment. He will ever after treat you as his dear friend." Christ will actually treat the saints as friends and family. But more than that, Christ will intimately communicate something of himself and his excellencies to them. Christ "will not keep them at a greater distance for his being in a state of exaltation; but he will rather take them into a state of exaltation. This will be the improvement Christ will make of his own glory, to make his beloved friends partakers with him, to glorify them in his glory."[147]

In heaven, the saints' "vital union" with Christ will be "perfect."[148] This has significant implications in one final area. For Edwards, being united with Christ means being united with God. Edwards expresses this doctrine in rather startling language. He begins by noting, "By your being united to Christ, you will have a more glorious union with an enjoyment of God the Father, than otherwise could be."[149] Edwards argues that since Christ is a divine-human person, being in intimate union with him allows one to participate in his intimate inner-trinitarian union with God:

> For being members of God's own Son, they are in a sort partakers of his relation to the Father: they are not only sons of God by regeneration, but by a kind of communion in the sonship of the eternal Son . . . So we being members of the Son, are partakers in our measure of the Father's love to the Son, and complacence in him . . . So we shall, according to our capacities, be partakers of the Son's enjoyment of God, and have his joy fulfilled in ourselves.[150]

Edwards ends the sermon with the striking statement that union with Christ admits one, in a manner of speaking, into God's inner-trinitarian life. When one is linked with the beautiful Christ, one is in intimate union with God's beauty and being. Christ "and his Father, and his people, should be as one society, one family; that the church should be as it were admitted into the society of the blessed Trinity."[151] Union with Christ admits one into the very society of the Trinity.

---

[147] "Excellency of Christ," Hickman, vol. 1, p. 689.
[148] Ibid.
[149] Ibid.
[150] Ibid.
[151] Ibid.

"The Excellency of Christ" is important for our understanding of Edward's idea of beauty. The sermon clearly shows Edwards' christocentric incarnational understanding of genuine religious experience. For Edwards, Christ is beauty incarnate. God's beauty in Christ is portrayed by Edwards as an elaborate tapestry of conjoined excellencies. Christ is excellent in his person, life, and work and in the application of those excellencies in the experience and life of the saints. It is through the incarnate Christ that one is able to apprehend the beauty of God. Further, Christ is paradigmatic for the experience of all of the saints in that the one who is filled with God's beauty inwardly will manifest that beauty outwardly. And importantly, when one is linked with Christ, God's beauty is actually experienced. Indeed one is, in a manner of speaking, admitted into God's beauty. These affirmations have significant implications: sainthood for Edwards involved not only an experience of God's beauty, but also a manifestation of that beauty.

"Proportioned Christians"

In his work *Religious Affections*, Edwards states that one of the positive signs of genuine religious experience is a manifestation of beauty in the life of the saint. In delineating the positive signs of the graciously affected person, he writes: "Another thing wherein those affections that are truly gracious and holy, differ from those that are false, is beautiful symmetry and proportion."[152] Saints, who through the sense of the heart have experienced God's beauty and have been given a new apprehension of divine beauty, are to manifest beauty in their affections. The life of the saint is to be a life of beauty experienced and portrayed. For Edwards, beauty, in the manifestation of a proportionality of the affections, is a distinctive characteristic of sainthood.

In one of a series of sermons based on I Corinthians 13, entitled *Charity and Its Fruits*, Edwards uses the phrase "proportioned Christians" to epitomize the description of the true saint. The title of the sermon is "Christian Graces Concatenated Together." The doctrine of the sermon is stated as: "There is a concatenation of the graces of Christianity."[153] Edwards describes how various graces are linked together, dependent on one another, and "implied one in another."[154] Saints should "endeavor that each grace that we have may testify to the genuineness of all our other graces, so that we may be

---

[152] *Religious Affections* in Yale 2, p. 365. For a more extended discussion of this important sign, see our discussion below of the tenth positive sign.
[153] On "concatenation," see Ramsey, Yale 8, pp. 326–338.
[154] "Christian Graces Concatenated Together," Yale 8, p. 330.

proportioned Christians, growing into the unity of the faith and of the knowledge of the Son of God, unto perfect men, unto the measure of the stature of the fullness of Christ."[155] "Proportioned Christians" are to manifest a "concatenation" of graces. There is to be a beauty of proportionality in their affections. The phrase "proportioned Christians" is reminiscent of a similar phrase employed by Edwards in his "Personal Narrative," in which describes his "burning desire to be in every thing a *complete Christian*."[156] In his *Treatise on Grace*, Edwards uses a related word to describe this interconnection of graces. He writes that "there is a consentanation of graces" in the life of a saint. One grace promotes and is implied in another.[157]

These terms—*concatenation*, *consentanation*, *complete Christians*, and *proportioned Christians*—belong to the language of beauty as descriptive of a proportioned manifestation of graces and affections. As Edwards attests in *Religious Affections*, at his discussion of the tenth positive sign, a visible manifestation of beauty is a distinguishing criterion of genuine religious experience. In their lives and affections, saints should evidence "beautiful symmetry and proportion."[158]

This beauty manifested in the saints is one of the beauties of heaven. In his sermon entitled "The Portion of the Righteous," Edwards states that the saints themselves will be more beautiful than heaven. Reflecting on the nature of the saint's resurrected body, he says:

> The body shall not only be raised in an exceeding strength, but in a wonderful beauty, for we are told that their bodies shall be like to Christ's glorious body. The greatest beauty that ever any human body appeared in in this world, is vile and base in comparison. The beauty of the bodies of the saints shall not only consist in the most lovely proportion of the features of their countenance and parts of their bodies, but in a semblance of the excellencies of their minds, which will appear exceedingly in their countenance.[159]

Related to the nature of the beauty of heaven, he continues:

> I would only observe, that however great the glory of [heaven] is, the glory of [the saints'] bodies will doubtless be far greater: for the place is made to be a dwelling-place for their glorious bodies, and the inhabitants will doubtless be more glorious than the habitation that is made

---

[155] "Christian Graces Concatenated Together," Yale 8, p. 338. Emphasis added.
[156] "Personal Narrative" in *Jonathan Edwards, Representative Selections With Introduction, Bibliography, and Notes*, ed. Clarence H. Faust and Thomas H. Johnson (New York: Hill and Wang, 1935; revised edition, 1962), p. 62. Emphasis added.
[157] *Treatise on Grace*, p. 40.
[158] *Religious Affections* in Yale 2, p. 365.
[159] "The Portion of the Righteous," in Hickman, vol. 2, p. 894.

for them: as the end is of greater value than the means. However bright heaven itself shall shine, the bodies of the saints themselves will shine far brighter, and appear far more beautiful.[160]

The spiritual beauty of the saints will be even more profound than their awesome physical beauty:

> the glory and beauty which God will put on their souls, will as far exceed the beauty of their bodies, as the beauty of their bodies will far exceed the beauty of the place . . . And so lovely will they be, that there will be more loveliness and beauty in the soul of one saint than in all the glory and beauty of the place put together.[161]

This is the case because the saints will manifest God's beauty shining from within them. Edwards writes, "they shall then shine with the glory of Christ reflected from them, without any thing to obscure the bright image."[162]

This profound manifestation of divine beauty in and through the saints is dynamic in nature. Even in heaven the saints will grow and intensify in their manifestation of beauty. In a miscellany entitled "Happiness," Edwards writes:

> How soon do earthly lovers come to an end of their discoveries of each other's beauty; how soon do they see all that is to be seen! Are they united as near as 'tis possible and have communion as intimate as possible? how soon do they come to the most endearing expressions of love that 'tis possible to give, so that no new ways can be invented, given or received. And how happy is that love, in which there is an eternal progress in all these things; wherein new beauties are continually discovered, and more and more loveliness, and in which we shall forever increase in beauty ourselves; where we shall be made capable of finding out and giving, and shall receive, more and more endearing expressions of love forever: our union will become more close, and communion more intimate.[163]

Those who have experienced God's beauty will themselves manifest beauty in both their earthly and heavenly lives.

Corporate Beauty

Beyond examining Edwards' understanding of the nature of religious experience in the life of the individual, it is important also to examine the extent to

---

[160] Ibid., pp. 897 and 898.
[161] Ibid., p. 898.
[162] Ibid., p. 898.
[163] Miscellany, #198, Yale 13, pp. 336 and 337.

which Christian experience by its very nature involves a tendency or disposition toward expression in saintly society. There is a corporate or communal dimension to religious experience related to Edwards' idea of beauty. The manifestation of beauty is not only one of the distinguishing characteristics of individual saints; it is an important quality of saintly society. Indeed beauty is at the heart of Edwards' social vision.

It has been part of the standard historiography to interpret Edwards as lacking a social vision beyond the concerns of the spiritual life.[164] More recent scholarship has altered that view. Perhaps the most comprehensive treatment of Edwards' social theory is that of Gerald R. McDermott in *One Holy and Happy Society: The Public Theology of Jonathan Edwards*. McDermott paints a portrait of Edwards' social vision of "one holy and happy society,"[165] relating this social vision to national covenant issues, and thus correcting previous interpretations of Edwards' view of the role of New England and America in the millennium.[166] McDermott delineates Edwards' millennial societal vision and demonstrates that Edwards had a keen interest in social issues for Northampton during his pastoral years there. Edwards preached on charity to the poor, economic justice, and political theory related to being both a community leader and a good citizen. According to McDermott, "Edwards practiced what he preached" in his own charitable giving and in advocacy for marginalized people such as women, native American Indians, youth, and others.[167] McDermott argues that it was Edwards' corporate millennial vision that added impetus to his developing emphasis on Christian practice as "the constitutive essence of Christian experience."[168]

Whether McDermott is correct in his assessment of the extent of Edwards' social vision, one thing is clear: the vocabulary of the language of beauty was

---

[164] Gerhard T. Alexis, "Jonathan Edwards and the Theocratic Ideal," *Church History* 35.3, (September, 1966) p. 329; and H. Richard Niebuhr, *The Kingdom of God in America* (New York: Harper and Row, Torchbooks, 1959), p. 123.

[165] Gerald R. McDermott, *One Holy and Happy Society: The Public Theology of Jonathan Edwards* (University Park: Pennsylvania State University Press, 1992). The title phrase "one holy and happy society" is found in Edwards' "Letter to a Correspondent in Scotland," Yale 5, p. 446.

[166] McDermott states that most students of Edwards have misread him related to the millennium's timetable and America's millennial role. According to McDermott, Edwards did not believe that the millennium was imminent. The millennium was hundreds of years in the future. What Edwards believed to be imminent was a period preparatory to the actual millennium. This period, Edwards speculated, may have been dawning with the New England revivals. McDermott's reading of Edwards helps to resolve some previously perceived inconsistencies within Edwards' thought. See pp. 50–63.

[167] McDermott, *One Holy*, pp. 45 and 160–165.

[168] Ibid., p. 99. McDermott writes, "those students of Edwards' social theory who claim that Edwards' millennialism discouraged serious engagement with history miss the implications of his ontology for the importance of temporality" (p. 100).

an important part of the expression of Edwards' millennial vision. For example, in the *Dissertation Concerning the End For Which God Created the World*, Edwards describes the eschatological union between God and God's people:

> The creature is no further happy with this happiness which God makes his ultimate end than he becomes one with God. The more happiness the greater union: when the happiness is perfect, the union is perfect. And as the happiness will be increasing to eternity, the union will become more and more strict and perfect; nearer and more like to that between God the Father and the Son; who are so united, that their interest is perfectly one.[169]

There is, according to Edwards, an actual experience of God's inner-trinitarian beauty and a union between the creature and God's being. The greater the union, the greater is the happiness. In the sermon "The Excellency of Christ," Edwards describes this union as a kind of entrance into God's inner-trinitarian fellowship. He writes "Christ has brought it to pass, that those whom the Father has given him should be brought into the household of God; that he and his Father, and his people, should be as one society, one family; that the Church should be as it were admitted into the society of the blessed Trinity."[170] That which is implied in the *Dissertation Concerning the End For Which God Created the World* is made explicit in the sermon: that is, that the union is of a corporate nature. It is the church which is, as it were, admitted into the society of God's inner-trinitarian being. It is the society of the saints, not just individual saints, which is in union with the society of God's being.

Further, the corporate or societal union is a dynamic union. It will increase and intensify throughout all eternity without ever becoming fully actualized. The union is one always in process, always becoming, never arriving:

> Let the most perfect union with God be represented by something at an infinite height above us; and the eternally increasing union of the saints with God, by something that is ascending constantly towards that infinite height, moving upwards with a given velocity; and that is to continue thus to move to all eternity. God who views the whole of this eternally increasing height views it as an infinite height. And if he has respect to it, and makes it his end, as in the whole of it, he has respect to it as an infinite height, though the time will never come when it can be said it has already arrived at this infinite height.[171]

It is this dynamic, progressive process of union between the society of God's

---

[169] *Dissertation Concerning the End*, Yale 8, pp. 533 and 534. On union see *Nature of True Virtue* in Yale 8, pp. 564 and 725; also see "Portion of the Righteous" in Hickman, vol. 2, p. 901.
[170] "The Excellency of Christ," Hickman, vol. 1, p. 689.
[171] *Dissertation Concerning the End*, Yale 8, p. 534.

being and the society of God's saints which is the eschatological goal of creation. God's disposition toward this union is, according to Edwards, the very reason for created existence. Edwards writes that "a disposition in God, as an original property of his nature, to an emanation of his own infinite fullness, was what excited him to create the world; and so that emanation itself was aimed at by him as a last end of the creation."[172] In heaven this union will be more fully actualized. Edwards' vision of the society of heaven was to serve as a model for societal life in this world.

For Edwards, heaven is a place of overwhelming beauty. The place itself is beautiful. However, each saint is even more beautiful than the beauty of the heavenly surroundings. Further, there is a corporate dimension to the beauty of heaven. In the sermon "Portion of the Righteous," Edwards states, "the saints in heaven shall all be one society, they shall be united together without any schism, there shall be a sweet harmony, and a perfect union."[173] The saints in heaven will be a "blessed family." This family will be like a healthy physical body: "this blessed family, being all united in one body, as having many members, shall all subserve and contribute to each other's happiness, as the members of a body that is in perfect health."[174]

Heavenly society will be one of beautiful harmony. There will be heavenly harmony in the actual singing of God's praises, "each one bearing his part in the heavenly melody." Edwards writes, "What a glorious harmony of celestial voices without number will that be, when the whole assembly of the upper world shall together lift up the praise of God on high!"[175] However, there will also be a heavenly harmony in the society of the saints and their love for each other. Especially contrasted with contentious jealousies and schisms in the earthly church, "there will be perfect harmony in that society" of heaven.[176]

THE BEAUTY OF ORDER

Edwards' vision of millennial society reflected his understanding of society in heaven. The millennium would usher in a beautiful society of peace, prosperity,

---

[172] Ibid., p. 435.
[173] "Portion of the Righteous," Hickman, vol. 2, p. 898.
[174] Ibid.
[175] Ibid.
[176] Ibid., pp. 898 and 902. On the theme of music, see Robert W. Jenson's chapter "The End" in *America's Theologian: A Recommendation of Jonathan Edwards* (New York and Oxford: Oxford University Press, 1988), pp. 177–185. Nowhere is Edwards' vision of the beauty and harmony of heavenly society more clearly pictured than in "Heaven is a World of Love." This is the concluding sermon in the series *Charity and Its Fruits* in Yale 8. Both Paul Ramsey and Wilson Kimnach believe the sermon to be one of Edwards' masterpieces of rhetorical power, rivaling if not surpassing the imagery of "Sinners in the Hands of an Angry God."

harmony, and order. For example, regarding the church during the millennial era, Edwards writes:

> [W]hen God's people in all different parts of the world, and the whole earth shall become more sensibly, as it were, one family, one holy and happy society, and all brethren, not only all united in one Head, but in greater affection, and in more mutual correspondence, and more visible and sensible union and fellowship in religious exercises, and the holy duties of the service of God; *and so that in this respect, the church on earth will become more like the blessed society in heaven, and vast assembly of saints and angels there.*[177]

Several components of heavenly society are present in his depiction of millennial communal life. In the millennium, there will be the unification of many different people. That unity will be in the form of a "visible and sensible union." There will be mutual caring and affection in corporate life, the whole earth being as "one family." Corporate life will reflect "one holy and happy society." This millennial vision is also stated by Edwards in his sermon series *A History of the Work of Redemption*. In that series, Edwards unfolds his philosophy of history as he graphically portrays the drama of redemption. In the twenty-seventh of thirty sermons, Edwards describes millennial society, especially the beauty which will be Christ's church. Note the language of beauty in the following description: "a time of excellent order in the church discipline and government shall be settled in his church; all the world shall be as one church, and one orderly, regular, beautiful society, one body, all the members in beautiful proportion . . . [T]he church of God shall be beautiful on these accounts, yea it will appear in perfection of beauty . . ."[178] For Edwards, the millennial church will be a beautiful corporate society.

That which is descriptive of the millennial church is also, for Edwards, descriptive of millennial society in general. Edwards' millennial social vision extends beyond matters that are expressly spiritual in nature. To be sure, the spiritual nature of millennial society is important. In the seventeenth sermon in *A History of the Work of Redemption*, Edwards states that the millennium will be a time of great spiritual advancement in the conversion of the heathen. This will also be a time of great increase in religious knowledge and a time of great holiness. But the blessings of the millennium will be more than spiritual in nature: millennial blessings will extend, in very specific ways, to society at large.

As will the church during the millennium, millennial society in general will exhibit beauty. The millennium will be "a time wherein the whole great society

---

[177] "Letter to a Correspondent in Scotland," Yale 5, p. 446. Emphasis added.
[178] *A History of the Work of Redemption*, Yale 9, p. 484.

shall appear in glorious beauty, in genuine amiable Christianity, and excellent order."[179] Society will show forth the beauty of cordial consent and union. Edwards writes, "and then shall all the world be united in peace and love in one amiable society, all nations, in all parts, on every side of the globe, shall then be knit together in sweet harmony . . ."[180]

There will be harmony, peace, and love throughout society. The millennium will especially be a time of worldwide peace. Edwards writes in *An Humble Attempt* that the millennium will be

> a time of wonderful union, and the most universal peace, love and sweet harmony wherein the nations shall "beat their swords into plowshares" . . . a time wherein the whole earth shall be united as one holy city, one heavenly family, men of all nations shall as it were dwell together, and sweetly correspond one with another as brethren . . .[181]

The millennium will also be a time of great prosperity. Prosperity will be seen not only in temporal wealth and an abundance of goods, but in "health, ease, quietness, pleasantness, wealth, great increase of children." The land will be fruitful and people will receive "all manner of tokens of God's presence, acceptance and favor."[182]

Another distinction of the millennium is that there will be a great increase in knowledge and technology. It has been noted above that for the church, spiritual knowledge will abound; but Edwards also envisioned an explosion of human knowledge in general. The millennium "will be a time of great light and knowledge. The present days are days of darkness in comparison of those days."[183] According to Edwards, new technologies are types of this future advancement of knowledge. In "Images of Divine Things," Edwards states: "the late invention of telescopes, whereby heavenly objects are brought so much nearer and made so much plainer to sight and such wonderful discoveries have been made in the heavens, is a type and forerunner of the great increase in the knowledge of heavenly things that shall be in the approaching glorious times of the Christian church."[184] This increase in knowledge and technology will lend itself to a spiritual purpose. Technology will facilitate daily life, Edwards believes, allowing more time and energy for spiritual pursuits.[185]

---

[179] *An Humble Attempt*, Yale 5, p. 339.
[180] *A History of the Work of Redemption*, Yale 9, p. 483.
[181] *An Humble Attempt*, Yale 5, p. 339.
[182] *A History of the Work of Redemption*, Yale 9, pp. 484 and 485.
[183] Ibid., p. 480.
[184] "Images of Divine Things," #146, Yale 11, p. 101.
[185] Miscellany, #262, Yale 13, p. 369. On other implications for this increase in knowledge, see miscellany entitled "Millennium," #26, in Yale 13, pp. 212 and 213.

Increasing knowledge and technology will aid in the development of a worldwide community of people and nations. Barriers will be broken down; the world will be one family. The millennium, according to Edwards, will not only be a time of significant spiritual beauty in union and harmony in the church, but society in general will benefit from worldwide peace, abundant prosperity, and expansive knowledge and technology, so that "the whole earth may be as one community."[186] Millennial society in all its dimensions will be beautiful.

THE BEAUTY OF UNION

The millennium and eschatology in general occupied a significant place in Edwards' theology. Similar to the expression of his vision for millennial society and the eschatological church was the expression of his vision for the church and society in general in his own time.[187] In *An Humble Attempt*, published in 1748, Edwards articulated his vision of the millennial church as a well ordered and beautiful society of peace and prosperity. The context of that work, however, was not merely to portray an eschatological vision; *An Humble Attempt* was an effort to help bring about the actualization of that vision for the church in Edwards' own day.

Edwards wrote *An Humble Attempt* as his contribution to the endeavor for a worldwide concert of prayer as a means of promoting revival. Based on the model of such a concert of prayer instituted by a group of Scottish ministers, Edwards endorsed the following as the concert's method of operation:

> After seeking to God by prayer for direction, they determined on the following method, as what they would conform to in their own practice, and propose to be practiced by others, for the two years next following, viz., to set apart some time on Saturday evening and Sabbath morning, every week, for the purpose aforesaid . . . and more solemnly, the first Tuesday of each quarter . . . either the whole day, or part of the day . . . the time to be spent either in private praying societies, or in public meetings, or alone in secret, as shall be found more practicable, or judged most convenient, by such as are willing in some way or other, to join in this affair.[188]

---

[186] Miscellany, #262, Yale 13, p. 369.
[187] On the importance of the millennium for Edwards, see John F. Wilson's "History, Redemption, and Millennium" in Nathan O. Hatch & Harry S. Stout, eds. *Jonathan Edwards and the American Experience* (New York and Oxford: Oxford University Press, 1988), p. 133.
[188] *An Humble Attempt*, Yale 5, p. 321.

The call was for definite days and periods of prayer for the revival of the church and society. Such a concerted effort using the means of prayer was an appropriate venture because scripture taught

> That it is a very suitable thing and well pleasing to God, for many people in different parts of the world, by express agreement, to come into visible union, in extraordinary, speedy, fervent and constant prayer, for those great effusions of the Holy Spirit, which shall bring on that advancement of Christ's church and Kingdom, that God has so often promised shall be in the latter age of the world.[189]

The concert of prayer was to be implemented by "express agreement." It would evidence a "visible union" of God's people. The means to the end of eschatological union would itself promote that union and agreement. Such union was not only an eschatological goal; the beauty of union in church and society was for Edwards a present goal toward which church and society should strive:

> How condecent, how beautiful, and of good tendency would it be, for multitudes of Christians, in various parts of the world, by explicit agreement, to unite in such prayer as is proposed to us. Union is one of the most amiable things, that pertains to human society; yea, 'tis one of the most beautiful and happy things on earth, which indeed makes earth most like heaven . . . hereby teaching us the moral lesson, that it becomes mankind all to be united as one family. And this is agreeable to the nations that God has given men, disposing them to society . . . Union is spoken of in scripture as the peculiar beauty of the Church of Christ . . . As 'tis the glory of the Church of Christ, that she, in all her members, however dispersed, is thus one, one holy society, one city, one family, one body, so it is very desirable that this union should be manifest, and become visible.[190]

There is much in this lengthy quotation that is important for our discussion. A tendency toward union as "agreeable to the nature that God has given men" is an important constitutive part of Edwards' understanding of the dispositional nature of being in general and human being in particular. Further, *union* as "the peculiar beauty of the church" must become manifest. Union is "one of the most beautiful and happy things on earth, which indeed makes earth most like heaven." The heavenly goal of eschatological union is a worthy goal for the present (to Edwards) this-worldly church and society. The same

---

[189] Ibid., p. 320.
[190] Ibid., p. 365.

thought is conveyed in a letter to an unidentified Scottish correspondent dated November 20, 1745:

> I hope the time is hastening, when God's people in the different parts of the world, and the whole earth shall become more sensibly, as it were, one family, one holy and happy society, and all brethren, not only all united in one Head, but in greater affection and in more mutual correspondence, and more visible and sensible union . . . and so that in this respect, the church on earth will become more like the blessed society in heaven, and vast assembly of saints and angels there.[191]

The blessed society of the eschatological community was the paradigm of communal life for church and society. *Union* in the eschatological community was a model for *union* in this-worldly society. Similar connections could be made for other aspects of eschatological communal life. For example, peace and prosperity, which were constitutive elements of millennial communal life, were goals toward which contemporary society should work. As we have seen, Edwards preached that there should not be division and contention in the church. Further, communal prosperity should be actualized through charity to the poor.[192] However, as important as the eschatological model was for Edwards' social theory, there was also an activistic social impulse in Edwards' dispositional philosophy of being and his idea of beauty.

"One Cannot Subsist Alone"

Being is, for Edwards, relational in nature. In his notebook "The Mind," he writes, "for being, if we examine narrowly, is nothing else but proportion."[193] Being must be proportionately related to other being. There is no such thing for Edwards as solitary existence. In the same notebook entry, Edwards succinctly offers the statement upon which so much of his philosophical theology, especially as it is related to beauty, is built. He says, "one alone, without any reference to any more, cannot be excellent; for in such a case there can be no manner of relation no way, and therefore, no such thing as consent."[194]

In a remarkably similar statement, Edwards explicates a social theory based on a relational philosophy of being. In a sermon entitled "Christian Charity: or The Duty of Charity to the Poor, Explained and Enforced," which he preached in 1733, Edwards states that charity to the poor is reasonable

---

[191] Yale 5, p. 446. Stephen Stein believes the correspondent to be John McLaurin of Glasgow. See p. 444, note 1.
[192] See sermon on "Christian Charity" and discussion below.
[193] "The Mind," Yale 6, p. 336.
[194] "The Mind," Yale 6, p. 337.

because all people are related in that all are made in the image of God. There is further relatedness in that all people have "the same nature, like faculties, like dispositions, like desires of good, like needs, like aversion to misery and are made of one blood." He continues, "And we are made to subsist by society and union one with another. God hath made us with such a nature, that we cannot subsist without the help of one another. Mankind in this respect are as members of the natural body, *one cannot subsist alone, without an union without the help of the rest*."[195] It is part of human nature that there be a society of union and mutual care. One cannot subsist alone; one alone cannot be excellent; for being is proportion.

Edwards states this principle in a similar fashion in *An Humble Attempt*. The lengthy quotation from that work cited above made clear that for Edwards, union is one of the most amiable, beautiful, and happy things on earth. God has created people in relation to one another, says Edwards, "hereby teaching us this moral lesson, that it becomes mankind all to be united as one family. And this is agreeable to the nature that God has given man, disposing them to society."[196] Because being is relational in nature, human beings are created to live in societal union. For Edwards, union implies mutual caring and consent. Therefore it is requisite from the very nature of being that people care for each other. This is the social theory expanded in the sermon on "Christian Charity." Here Edwards teaches that mankind must "love their neighbors." He further notes how inconsistent a selfish spirit is to the system of being:

> A selfish spirit is very unsuitable to the nature and state of mankind. He who is all for himself, and none for his neighbors, deserves to be cut off from the benefit of human society, and be turned out among wild beasts, to subsist by himself as well as he can. A private niggardly spirit is more suitable for wolves, and other beasts of prey, than for human beings.[197]

Further, Edwards made concern for the physical well-being of others one of the signs of genuine religion. In the tenth positive sign recorded in *Religious Affections*, which states that gracious affections will evidence "beautiful symmetry and proportion," Edwards says that some people, in a very disproportionate fashion,

---

[195] "Christian Charity: or The Duty of Charity to the Poor, Explained and Enforced" in Hickman, vol. 2, p. 164. Emphasis added.
[196] *An Humble Attempt*, Yale 5, pp. 324 and 365.
[197] "Christian Charity: or The Duty of Charity to the Poor, Explained and Enforced" in Hickman, vol. 2, pp. 164 and 165.

pretend a great love to men's souls; that are not compassionate and charitable towards their bodies, the making a great show of love, pity and distress for souls, costs 'em nothing; but in order to show mercy to men's bodies, they must part with money out of their pockets. But a true Christian love to our brethren extends both to their souls and bodies.[198]

Edwards was concerned not just for people's spiritual needs; beautiful and proportionate affections, he believed, must evidence concern for both souls and bodies.[199]

For Edwards, sainthood began with an experience of God's beauty through the sense of the heart. It was to be a life in which that beauty would become manifested through the saints' proportioned affections. Further, Edwards used the vocabulary of the language of beauty in the expression of a corporate societal vision. For Edwards, it was not only the structure of individual religious life; it was the structure of corporate religious experience and communal life.

---

[198] *Religious Affections* in Yale 2, p. 369.
[199] Mark Valeri states that for Edwards, "giving to charity was one of the few truly reliable, visible signs of sainthood." "The Economic Thought of Jonathan Edwards," *Church History* 60.1 (March, 1991), p. 46.

IV

Signs of Beauty

Near the end of the decade in which the revivals called the Great Awakening came to New England and other colonies, Edwards wrote the following: "There are two ways of representing and recommending true religion and virtue to the world, which God hath made use of: the one is by doctrine and precept; the other is by instance and example."[200] When he wrote these words, Edwards had already composed a formidable corpus of works chronicling and defending the revivals. In these works he made use of these revivals in two ways. He wrote several treatises analyzing the religion of the revivals in light of the theological nature of his understanding of genuine religious experience. Some of those treatises contained "real life" case studies of people who had been affected by the revivals.

In this chapter and the next, that core of works associated with the revivals and Edwards' analyses of genuine religious experience will be examined. It is relevant to examine not only Edwards' keen theological analyses contained in these works, but also the case examples which Edwards offered in order to validate the theology he expounded. The importance of the idea of beauty in Edwards' understanding of genuine religious experience is evident in both theological analysis and case examples. The focus here is on doctrine—Edwards' theory of religious experience. For Edwards, as we shall see, "Christian experience" is an experience of beauty which is manifested in beautiful affections.

RELIGIOUS AFFECTIONS

In 1746 Edwards published what was to be his classic analysis of the psychology of religious experience, entitled *Religious Affections*. This treatise was

---

[200] *The Life of David Brainerd*, Yale 7, p. 89.

based on a sermon series that Edwards had preached earlier at Northampton. By the time he published *Religious Affections*, Edwards had already written and published the core of his apologetic works on the revival. With one notable exception in the David Brainerd diary (1749), Edwards had presented the historical chronology and descriptive case studies as part of his apologetic task. In *Religious Affections*, Edwards presented a sustained theological analysis of religious experience. He sought to answer the questions with which he begins the preface: "What are the distinguishing qualifications of those that are in favor with God, and entitled to his eternal rewards? Or, which comes to the same thing, what is the nature of true religion."[201]

One of the key factors in *Religious Affections*, especially as related to the earlier treatise, is Edwards' use of signs. The discussion of the important miscellany #782 noted that Edwards, following John Locke, viewed signs as necessary to thought and knowledge. The mind, said Edwards, could not have actual ideas of every idea presented to it—for example, in reading a page of a book. The mind must substitute and, according to Edwards, the mind habitually does substitute signs for those ideas. There is a "kind of mental reading" by which the mind connects ideas by their signs.[202] In *Religious Affections*, written not long after miscellany #782, Edwards applies the epistemological nature of "sign" to his psychology of religious experience. Edwards is no longer concerned with words as signs, as he was in miscellany #782. In the treatise, he is concerned with "affections" as signs and with the capability of reading such signs correctly. In his editor's introduction to the Yale series edition of *Religious Affections*, John E. Smith writes:

> Turning to the meaning of sign in the positive sense, we must understand a sign to be a mark through which the presence of the divine Spirit can be known. Edwards does not say that we *infer* the presence of God's grace using signs as a basis; he does in fact, leave that relationship vague. It is best to suppose that the sign "points to" the activity of the Spirit, especially when we consider the matter from the side of our human process of knowing. Taken apart from its evidential force, however, a sign must be understood as the very presence of the Spirit, since it is the working of divine grace in the heart of the believer.[203]

According to Smith, gracious affections constitute positive signs, indicating the presence of the Holy Spirit. In the language of the treatise, it may be said that through the sense of the heart, the saint experiences God's beauty, and

---

[201] *Religious Affections*, Yale 2, p. 84.
[202] Miscellany, #782, in Townsend, p. 118.
[203] Smith, Yale 2, p. 23.

such an experience may be a positive sign of genuine religion. Indeed for Edwards, as we shall see, one such sign is beauty itself in the form of a symmetry and proportionality of affections.

Edwards begins *Religious Affections* by announcing a text of scripture, 1 Pet. 1:8, which in the King James Version reads: "Whom having not seen, ye love: in whom, though now ye see him not, yet believing, ye rejoice with joy unspeakable, and full of glory." Edwards, in sermonic fashion, notes that at the time these words were written, the New Testament church was undergoing persecution. He says that such trials and persecutions have a beneficial effect on "true religion" in that

> they not only manifest the truth of it, but they make its genuine beauty and amiableness remarkably to appear. True virtue never appears so lovely, as when it is most oppressed: and the divine excellency of real Christianity, is never exhibited with such advantage, as when under the greatest trials: then it is that true faith appears much more precious than gold; and upon this account, is found to praise, and honor, and glory.[204]

That which Edwards terms "true religion," "true virtue," "real Christianity," and "true faith" manifests itself under trial. Here Edwards anticipates an argument in his *The Nature of True Virtue*, in which he equates true virtue with love of Being in general.

In sermonic fashion Edwards announces the doctrine as: "True religion, in great part, consists in holy affections."[205] He notes from the text the "affections" of love and joy and the excellency of such characteristics. In the age of the apostles, true religion was manifested "most in its genuine excellency and native beauty, and was found to praise, and honor, and glory; [the apostle] singles out the religious affections of love and joy, that were then in exercise in them: these are the exercises of religion he takes note of, wherein their religion did thus appear true and pure, and is proper glory."[206]

In defining what he means by the affections, Edwards says that "affections are no other, than the more vigorous and sensible exercises of the inclination and the will of the soul."[207] By way of clarification, Edwards says that the soul has two faculties. The *understanding* is the faculty through which the soul exercises perception, speculation, discernment, and judgment. The second faculty may be labeled by several different terms. It is the *inclination* by which

---

[204] *Religious Affections*, Yale 2, p. 93.
[205] Ibid., 95.
[206] Ibid.
[207] Ibid., p. 96.

the soul exercises pleasure or displeasure, inclination or disinclination. By way of further clarification: as this faculty "has respect to the actions that are determined and governed by it, is called the *will*: and the *mind*, with regard to the exercise of this faculty, is often called the *heart*."[208] It is this faculty, variously termed the inclination, will, or heart, that involves the affections. Edwards says that "they are these more vigorous and sensible exercises of this faculty, that are called the *affections*."[209] Edwards is careful to note that one should not be too technical in the distinction between how this faculty relates to the mind and will. "Heart" applies to all that is mind, including will and understanding. The affections involve the whole person as an involved participant. He is also careful to differentiate the affections from passions which are sudden and more violent and which overpower the mind.[210]

Affectionate or affective religion is the opposite of "lukewarmness." There can be no genuine religion, says Edwards, unless one's heart is deeply affected by the things of religion.[211] This is the religion portrayed in the scriptures. And the scriptures portray love as "the chief of the affections, and the father of all other affections."[212] Edwards contends that "[f]rom a vigorous, affectionate, and fervent love to God, will necessarily arise other religious affections."[213] He writes:

> [H]ence will arise an intense hatred and abhorrence of sin, fear of sin, and a dread of God's displeasure, gratitude to God for his goodness, complacence and joy in God when God is graciously and sensibly present, and grief when he is absent, and a joyful hope when a future enjoyment of God is expected and a fervent zeal for the glory of God. And in like manner, from a fervent love to men, will arise all other virtuous affections towards men.[214]

In the language of the treatise, love, which is the highest form of beauty, is an intensely and complexly beautiful religious affection.

In stressing the importance of the affections, Edwards notes several biblical examples of affective religion, including David, the apostle Paul, and Jesus. True affectionate religion produces a strong habit of holy affections. There must be the light of understanding coupled with the heat of an affected heart. This latter part is especially important:

---

[208] Ibid.
[209] Ibid., p. 97.
[210] Ibid., p. 98.
[211] Ibid., p. 102.
[212] Ibid., p. 106.
[213] Ibid., p. 108.
[214] Ibid.

> He who has no religious affection, is in a state of spiritual death, and is wholly destitute of the powerful, quickening, saving influence of the Spirit of God upon his heart. As there is no true religion, where there is nothing else but affection; so there is no true religion where there is no religious affection. As on the one hand, there must be light in the understanding, as well as an affected and fervent heart, where there is heat without light, there can be nothing divine or heavenly in that heart; so on the other hand, where there is a kind of light without heat, a head stored with notions and speculations, with a cold and unaffected heart, there can be nothing divine in that light, that knowledge is no true spiritual knowledge of divine things.[215]

True religion includes both light and heat, knowledge and affection. Genuine religious experience must include both pairings. For "if the great things of religion are rightly understood, they will affect the heart."[216]

Edwards has deliberately taken the middle ground between enthusiasts and rationalists. He notes that there may indeed be false affections and that passions are not affections. Having a great deal of religious affection does not necessarily prove that the religious experience is genuine. Having no affection, however, is a sure sign of the absence of true religion. Edwards calls upon critics of the revivals to understand that "the right way, is not to reject all affections, nor to approve all; but to distinguish between affections, approving some and rejecting others; separating between the wheat and the chaff, the gold and the dross, the precious and the vile."[217] It is those distinctions which Edwards proceeds to analyze.

NEGATIVE SIGNS

The treatise's second section is entitled: "Shewing what are no certain signs that religious affections are true, gracious or that they are not." One such inconclusive sign is "that religious affections are very great, or raised very high."[218] The intensity of the affections does not guarantee their authenticity, nor does the intensity of the bodily effects which may accompany them. Physiological effects are the second inconclusive sign.[219] Conversing about religion, even in a manner that is "fluent, fervent and abundant," is the third negative sign.[220] Fourth, "'Tis no sign that affections are gracious, or that

---

[215] Ibid., p. 120.
[216] Ibid.
[217] Ibid., p. 121.
[218] Ibid., p. 127.
[219] Ibid., p. 131.
[220] Ibid., p. 135.

they are otherwise, that persons did not make 'em themselves, or excite 'em of their own contrivance, and by their own strength."[221] In the discussion of these negative signs, Edwards cautions against the "enthusiastical" notion that the Holy Spirit works apart from established means. At the same time, he upholds the sovereign nature of God's grace to work freely according to God's will. God's sovereignty and gracious freedom must not be presumed upon. He writes that for people "to expect to receive the saving influences of the Spirit of God, while they neglect a diligent improvement of the appointed means of grace, is unreasonable presumption."[222] However, salvation can never be the automatic end of a pursuit through the means of grace, for

> 'tis God's manner, in the great works of his power and mercy which he works for his people, in ordering things so, as to make his hand visible, and his power conspicuous, and men's dependence on him most evident, that no flesh should glory in his presence, that God alone might be exalted, and that the excellency of the power and might be of God and not of man, and that Christ's power might be manifested in our weakness, and none might say mine own hand hath saved me.[223]

Religious affections are inconclusive even if texts of scripture are "brought suddenly and wonderfully to mind";[224] the devil can also quote scripture.[225] Further, there may even be the "appearance of love" in the affections, without their being salvific.[226] There may be a variety of affections accompanying one another and still the affections may not be gracious. Edwards says that what is lacking in this case is the beauty and "symmetry of parts" that he will later identify as one of the positive signs.[227] Edwards says that "as men, while in a state of nature are capable of a resemblance of all kinds of religious affections, so nothing hinders but that they may have many together."[228] As divine love is the source of genuine affections, so false affections can flow from a counterfeit love.[229]

The eighth negative sign addresses an issue that had long been a part of Edwards' New England Puritan heritage: "Nothing can certainly be determined

---

[221] Ibid., p. 138.
[222] Ibid.
[223] Ibid., pp. 139 and 140.
[224] Ibid., p. 143.
[225] Ibid., p. 144.
[226] Ibid., p. 146. This is the sixth negative sign.
[227] *Religious Affections*, Yale 2, p. 147. This is the seventh negative sign. For beauty as the tenth positive sign, see our discussion below.
[228] *Religious Affections*, Yale 2, p. 148.
[229] Ibid., p. 150.

concerning the nature of the affections by this, that comforts and joys seem to follow awakenings and convictions of conscience, in a *certain-order*."[230] Since the early years of New England Puritanism, the issue of whether there were certain preparatory steps to salvation and the particular order of those steps had been debated. The antinomian controversy of the seventeenth century first brought the conflict to light. Puritan divines such as Thomas Shepherd and Thomas Hooker labored to explicate in great detail the notion of the *ordo salutis* or the order of salvation. Although, as John Gerstner has demonstrated, Edwards preached the responsibility of preparation, he nevertheless refused to subscribe to a formula for salvation. He said that the devil can counterfeit preparatory steps. Their order could also be duplicated. There is no rule, says Edwards, regarding how far along the preparatory road the Spirit may lead a person without bestowing salvation. Further, pastoral experience had shown Edwards that the delineation of a certain order of preparatory experience was not a "certain sign of grace."[231] Edwards declares: "'Tis to be feared that some have gone too far towards directing the Spirit of the Lord, and marking out his footsteps for him, and limiting him to certain steps and methods."[232]

The ninth negative sign is that people are disposed "to spend much time in religion, and to be zealously engaged in the external duties of worship."[233] That people are also disposed to praise and glorify God is the tenth negative sign.[234] Even a sense of assurance of salvation is not a conclusive sign of gracious affections. Edwards identifies the eleventh inconclusive sign as "'Tis no sign that affections are right, or that they are wrong, that they make persons that have them exceeding confident that what they experience is divine, and that they are in a good estate."[235] Edwards affirms that saints may indeed have a sense of assurance of salvation or "an assured hope of eternal life, while being here upon earth." Indeed, "all Christians are directed to give all diligence to make their election sure."[236] However, such assurance is not in itself evidence of gracious affections. In some deceived "hypocrites," their ground of assurance is the very sort of inconclusive experiences which Edwards has already identified—for example, revelations accompanied by texts of scriptures.[237]

Edwards discusses the supposed possibility of a person living by faith apart

---

[230] Ibid., p. 151.
[231] Ibid., pp. 158–160. See Gerstner, *Steps to Salvation*.
[232] *Religious Affections*, Yale 2, p. 162.
[233] Ibid., p. 163.
[234] Ibid., p. 165.
[235] Ibid., p. 167.
[236] Ibid., p. 169.
[237] Ibid., p. 173.

from an experience of God and finding assurance of salvation by this faith. He insists that it is not faith which is salvific. Faith in this sense could be viewed as a human work, thus resulting in a works-righteousness. Rather, the focus of one's "gaze" is not to be one's faith or one's experience. It is Christ who saves, and one's attention must always be God-ward and Christ-ward; God's beauty should be the focus of one's gaze. He says: "[I]nstead of keeping their eyes on God's glory, and Christ's excellency, they turn their eyes off these objects without them, onto themselves, to entertain their minds, by viewing their own attainments and high experiences . . . [T]his is living on experiences and not on Christ."[238] Basing one's assurance on one's faith experience is "more abominable in God's sight than the gross immoralities of those who make no pretence of religion."[239]

The twelfth and last negative sign reads: "Nothing can be certainly concluded concerning the nature of religious affections, that any are the subject of, from this, that the outward manifestations of them, and the relations persons give of them, are very affecting and pleasing to the truly godly, and such as greatly gain their charity, and win their hearts."[240] True saints do not have the ability to discern the spiritual condition of others. One of the particularly irksome practices of enthusiasts was that of judging other believers by a claimed immediate revelation of their condition.[241] Edwards categorically rejects such judging as prideful arrogance.

Positive Signs

Section three is by far the lengthiest section of the treatise. In it Edwards discusses twelve positive signs by which gracious affections may be known. Before entering into a discussion of the first positive sign, Edwards clarifies the purpose of such a discussion. He explains how the signs should not be used. He states that he is "far from undertaking to give such signs of gracious affections, as shall be sufficient to enable any certainty to distinguish true affections from false in others; or to determine positively which of their neighbors are true professors, and which are hypocrites."[242] The positive signs will not yield a certitude in discriminating knowledge of the condition of the soul of others.

Second, the signs cannot be certain evidence for one's own assurance of salvation. This is especially the case when one's faith, although genuine, may

---

[238] Ibid., pp. 180 and 181.
[239] Ibid., p. 181
[240] Ibid.
[241] Ibid., p. 187.
[242] Ibid., p. 193.

be weak. The eyes of sinful humanity are conditioned by sin. Therefore, "men in a corrupt and carnal frame, have their spiritual senses in but poor plight for judging and distinguishing spiritual things."[243] As Edwards will explicate under the discussion of the twelfth positive sign, practice is the best barometer for assurance. Here he says that "assurance is not to be obtained so much by self-examination, as by action."[244] Edwards continues that he is "far from pretending to lay down any such rules, as shall be sufficient of themselves, without other means, to enable all true saints to see their good state, or as supposing they should be the principal means of their satisfaction."[245] While seeking signs that are generally discriminating of genuine religious experience, Edwards is careful in the application of those signs. This is especially the case regarding the certitude of knowledge gained through them.

The first positive sign is: "Affections that are truly spiritual and gracious, do arise from those influences and operations on the heart, which are *spiritual, supernatural and divine.*"[246] Such designations distinguish the salvific work of the Holy Spirit from that which is described as *natural*. The difference as noted in miscellany #782 is that of the Spirit's assisting work versus the Spirit as infused in a person's life—the difference between the Spirit working on someone versus in someone. In describing this effect upon the saint, Edwards writes that "the Spirit of God is given to true saints to dwell in them, as his proper lasting abode; and to influence their hearts, as a principle of new nature, or as a divine supernatural spring of life and action."[247]

Edwards illustrates from nature, using water and light. He says that the saints do not merely drink the living water of the Holy Spirit, "but this living water becomes a well or fountain of water in the soul . . . and thus becomes a principle of life in them." Likewise, he continues, the light of Christ, the "Sun of Righteousness," doesn't just shine upon the saints, "but is so communicated to them that they shine also, and become little images of that Sun which shines upon them." The saints, themselves, become a "lightsome body."[248]

It is this indwelling presence of God's Holy Spirit that produces holy affections:

> The Spirit of God so dwells in the hearts of the saints, that he there, as a seed or spring of life, exerts and communicates himself, in this his sweet and divine nature, *making the soul a partaker of God's beauty* and Christ's

---

[243] Ibid., p. 195.
[244] Ibid.
[245] Ibid., p. 196.
[246] Ibid., p. 197.
[247] Ibid., p. 200.
[248] Ibid., pp. 200 and 201. Edwards refers to the life-giving sap of a tree as another illustration.

joy, so that the saint has truly fellowship with the Father, and with his Son Jesus Christ, in thus having the communion or participation of the Holy Ghost.[249]

In the vocabulary of the language of beauty it may be said that it is the saint's experience of God's beauty, in the person of the Holy Spirit, that is the foundation of all gracious affections. Edwards is careful to stress that although the saints are "partakers of the divine nature," they are not "made partakers of the essence of God." They are not "Godded with God" or "Christed with Christ." Rather they experience God's fullness or "God's spiritual beauty and happiness" according to their capacity.[250] The important point, however, is that true saints actually experience God's beauty.

In his discussion of the first positive sign, Edwards introduces the concept of the sense of the heart. He will more fully explicate that concept under the discussion of additional positive signs. Here, however, he begins to describe "what some metaphysicians call a new simple idea."[251] Related to the saints, he says, "there is a new inward perception or sensation of their minds, entirely different in its nature and kind, from anything that ever their minds were the subjects of before they were sanctified."[252] In regeneration the Holy Spirit gives a new spiritual sense or "a principle of new kind of perception or spiritual sensation."[253] This new mode of spiritual sensibility, while it is above and distinct from natural ability, is not a new faculty: "So this new spiritual sense is not a new faculty of understanding, but it is a new foundation laid in the nature of the soul, for a new kind of exercises of the same faculty of understanding."[254] Accompanying this new spiritual sensibility is a new habit or disposition. This "new holy disposition of heart that attends the new sense, is not a new faculty of will, but a foundation laid the nature of the soul, for a new kind of exercise of the same faculty of will."[255] After introducing these principles, Edwards undertakes a lengthy discussion showing how a number of the negative signs fall short of this spiritual disposition and sensibility.

The second positive sign is: "The first objective ground of gracious affections, is the transcendently excellent and amiable nature of divine things, as they are in themselves; and not any conceived relation they bear to self, or self-interest."[256] Edwards notes that what makes any person or creature lovely

[249] Ibid., p. 201.
[250] Ibid., p. 203.
[251] Ibid., p. 205.
[252] Ibid.
[253] Ibid.
[254] Ibid., p. 206.
[255] Ibid.
[256] Ibid., p. 240.

is that person's excellency or beauty. Similarly, God is lovely and worthy of love because God is infinitely excellent. God's nature is "infinite beauty, brightness, and glory itself."[257] Edwards argues that a genuine love for God must be based upon God's beauty and excellency, not on any sort of self-interested love. Contrasted with self-interested love, Edwards says of the saint's love for God that "[t]hey don't first see that God loves them, and then that he is lovely; but they first see that God is lovely and that Christ is excellent and glorious, and their hearts are first captivated with this view . . . and then, consequentially, they see God's love, and great favor to them."[258] The affections of the saints "begin with God," whereas "false affections begin with self."[259]

Here, it is important to note again the foundational role of the idea of beauty in Edwards' understanding of the nature of religious experience. An experience of God's beauty through the sense of the heart is not only the defining experience of sainthood, but a love of God's beauty is the primary religious affection and the foundation of all other genuine affections.

In the third positive sign, Edwards clarifies that foundation. The third sign is: "Those affections that are truly holy, are primarily founded on the loveliness of the moral excellency of divine things. Or (to express it otherwise), a love to divine things for the beauty and sweetness of their moral excellency, is the first beginning and spring of all holy affections."[260] It is the moral beauty of divine things that is the foundation of the saint's love. By the moral beauty of God, Edwards means the beauty of God's attributes exercised as a moral agent, most especially in holiness.[261] By broader application Edwards states that "holiness comprehends all the true moral excellency of intelligent beings: there is no other virtue, but real holiness."[262] Or, expressed another way, "the true beauty and loveliness of all intelligent beings does primarily and most especially consist in their moral excellency or holiness." A true love for God, therefore, says Edwards, "must begin with a delight in his holiness . . . for no other attribute is truly lovely without this."[263]

Further, it is the beauty of holiness that the sense of the heart allows one to see:

---

[257] Ibid., p. 242.
[258] Ibid., p. 246.
[259] Ibid.
[260] Ibid., pp. 253 and 254. John E. Smith rightly calls this sign "the aesthetic dimension" of religious experience for Edwards. See his *Jonathan Edwards, Puritan, Preacher and Philosopher*, p. 40.
[261] *Religious Affections*, Yale 2, p. 255.
[262] Ibid.
[263] Ibid., p. 257. Edwards also states, "Holy persons, in the exercise of holy affections, do love divine things primarily for their holiness." See p. 256.

> [T]he beauty of holiness is that thing in spiritual and divine things, which is perceived by this spiritual sense, that is so diverse from all that natural men perceive in them: this kind of beauty is the quality that is the immediate object of this spiritual sense: this is the sweetness that is the proper object of this spiritual taste.[264]

It is an apprehension of God's moral beauty which sovereignly draws a person to God. Edwards says that an apprehension of God's beauty

> will melt and humble the hearts of men, and wean them from the world, and draw them to God, and effectually change them. A sight of the awful greatness of God may overpower men's strength, and be more than they can endure; but if the moral beauty of God be hid, the enmity of the heart will remain in its full strength, no love will be enkindled, all will not be effectual to gain the will, but that remain inflexible.[265]

A perception of God's attributes may make a great impression upon a person. But without a perception of God's moral beauty the impression will not be effectual. However,"the first glimpse of the moral and spiritual glory of God shining into the heart, produces all these effects, as it were with omnipotent power, which nothing can withstand."[266]

The sense of the heart is a sensibility of beauty. Through the sense of the heart divine beauty is experienced and perceived. It is this new sensibility of divine beauty that produces in the saints a new disposition toward holiness and holy affections. Beauty is the foundation of all holy affections.

In the discussion of the fourth positive sign Edwards begins to expand the concept he introduced in his exposition of the first positive sign as the new simple idea. Here he uses the terminology of his important epistemological concept of the sense of the heart. The fourth sign reads: "Gracious affections do arise from the mind's being enlightened, rightly and spiritually to understand or apprehend divine things."[267] In the discussion of miscellany #782 and Edwards' important concept of the sense of the heart, it was noted that the sense of the heart as related to religious experience involved both a new order of perception (sense of the mind) and a new disposition or habit of heart. Both were seen as accompanying the actual infusion of God's Holy Spirit. In *Religious Affections*, Edwards again notes the connection in any genuine religious experience between head and heart. Gracious affections are not the product of passion or strong religious experiences divorced from religious

---

[264] *Religious Affections*, Yale 2, p. 260.
[265] Ibid., pp. 264 and 265.
[266] Ibid., p. 265.
[267] Ibid., p. 266.

knowledge: "Holy affections are not heat without light; but evermore arise from some information of the understanding, some spiritual instruction that the mind receives, some light or actual knowledge."[268]

Some religious knowledge may come as a result of awakening or from the "common illuminations of the Spirit of God."[269] Such knowledge is Spirit-assisted knowledge, an enhancement of natural principles and abilities. The knowledge described as gracious and salvific, however, is above nature: "[T]here is such a thing . . . as a spiritual, supernatural understanding of divine things, that is peculiar to the saints, and which those who are not saints have nothing of."[270]

At regeneration saints receive a new spiritual sense. Edwards reminds his readers that the immediate object of this new sense is "the supreme beauty and excellency of the nature of divine things, as they are in themselves."[271] All spiritual understanding consists "in a sense of the heart, of the supreme beauty and sweetness of the holiness or moral perfection of divine things, together with all that discerning and knowledge of things of religion, that depends upon and flows from such a sense." Edwards succinctly states that "spiritual understanding consists primarily in a sense of heart of that spiritual beauty."[272] After noting the difference between speculative knowledge and knowledge derived through the sense of the heart "wherein the mind doesn't only speculate and behold, but relishes and feels," Edwards repeats the assertion that "spiritual understanding primarily consists in the sense, or taste of the moral beauty of divine things."[273] Once this spiritual beauty is perceived, the soul "as it were opens a new world to its view."[274] Having once apprehended the beauty of God, which Edwards calls "the divinity of Divinity," the beauty of all other divine things may be seen.

The sense of the heart is an aesthetic experience of the deepest sort. It is an actual infusion of God's beauty in the person of the Holy Spirit. Further, the first result of this experience is a sense, an apprehension of God's beauty. The sense of the heart is both a sense of the mind and an actual sensible experience of God's beauty. It is both a tasting and a seeing of beauty. It involves both the will and the understanding, the heart and the head.[275]

---

[268] Ibid.
[269] Ibid., p. 270.
[270] Ibid.
[271] Ibid., p. 271.
[272] Ibid., p. 272.
[273] Ibid., pp. 272 and 273.
[274] Ibid., p. 273.
[275] John E. Smith, I think rightly, states that this integration was something Edwards' critics, e.g., Charles Chauncy, never quite grasped. See his *Jonathan Edwards, Puritan, Preacher and Philosopher*, pp. 41 and 42.

Through his discussion of the first four positive signs Edwards established the foundation for gracious affections as a spiritual experience and apprehension of God's beauty. He next proceeds to delineate the product of such experience and apprehension—the affections themselves. The fifth positive sign is: "Truly gracious affections are attended with a reasonable and spiritual conviction of the judgment, of the reality and certainty of divine things."[276] The beauty or excellency of divine things is one of the clearest evidences of their divinity. A person who, through the sense of the heart, has a view or sense of God's beauty has the genuineness of that experience confirmed by the beauty itself apprehended: "the divine glory and beauty of divine things is in itself, real evidence of their divinity, and the most direct and strong evidence."[277] Divine beauty produces an intuitive, self-evident testimony to its divinity, and thus its experiential authenticity.

Here Edwards also introduces another important aspect of the experience of beauty. The experience of God's beauty, through the sense of the heart, produces an apprehension of seeming antithetical religious sensations:

> As soon as ever the eyes are opened to behold the holy beauty and amiableness that is in divine things, a multitude of most important doctrines of the gospel, that depend upon it (which all appear strange and dark to natural men), are at once seen to be true. As for instance, hereby appears the truth of what the Word of God declares concerning the exceeding evil of sin; for the same eye that discerns the transcendent beauty of holiness, necessarily therein sees the exceeding odiousness of sin: the same taste which relishes the sweetness of true moral good, tastes the bitterness of moral evil.[278]

An experience of God's beauty necessarily involves a sensibility of one's sinfulness. Further, Edwards asserts, an apprehension of divine beauty assists the saint to a perception of the reasonableness of Christianity in ways superior to the conviction through irregularities and revelations associated with enthusiasm.

The next positive signs further delineate the various kinds of affections that should accompany genuine religious experience. At sign six Edwards writes: "Gracious affections are attended with evangelical humiliation."[279] Here Edwards, drawing on his Puritan heritage, makes a distinction between "legal" and "evangelical" humiliation. The former is the kind of humiliation which people in a natural state experience. It is a Spirit-assisted conviction of

---

[276] *Religious Affections*, Yale 2, p. 291.
[277] Ibid., p. 298.
[278] Ibid., p. 301.
[279] Ibid., p. 311.

sin and sensibility of the things of religion. It is the kind asserted by "hypocrites" who appear to have genuine religion but do not. It ultimately produces only despair. It contributes to spiritual pride and false assurance. One might say that there is no beauty in legal humiliation. It is not efficacious.

Evangelical humiliation, however, is the product of the gracious and efficacious operations of the Holy Spirit "implanting and exercising supernatural and divine principles." It arises from a sense of the transcendent beauty of divine things in their moral qualities."[280] Accompanied with this sensibility of the beauty of divine things is the sensibility of the odiousness of sin and a person's own sinful condition. Without despairing, people who experience evangelical humiliation are "brought sweetly to yield, and fully and with delight to prostrate themselves at the feet of God."[281]

The seventh positive sign states: "Another thing, wherein gracious affections are distinguished from others is, that they are attended with a change of nature."[282] Here Edwards shows that the experience of God's beauty is a transforming experience: "The soul is deeply affected by these discoveries and so affected as to be transformed."[283] Edwards examines the nature of conversion noting that the presence of the Holy Spirit in the soul imparts a new nature. Further, this new nature will evidence itself in holiness.[284]

Positive signs eight and nine portray something of what the new nature is to look like. Sign eight states: "Truly gracious affections differ from those affections that are false and delusive, in that they tend to, and are attended with the lamblike, dovelike spirit and temper of Jesus Christ."[285] Edwards says that the new nature produces "such a spirit of love, meekness, quietness, forgiveness and mercy, as appeared in Christ."[286] In a similar fashion he says at the ninth sign: "Gracious affections soften the heart, and are attended and followed with a Christian tenderness of Spirit."[287] In discussing these particular signs, Edwards speaks directly against much of the violent, passionate, combative, and critical attitudes present in some extremists. Critics of the revivals had associated these attitudes with the revivals as a whole.

His discussion of the tenth positive sign particularly expresses the importance of the idea of beauty in Edwards' understanding of the nature of genuine

---

[280] Ibid.
[281] Ibid., p. 312.
[282] Ibid., p. 340.
[283] Ibid.
[284] Here Edwards is anticipating much of what he will describe under the twelfth positive sign and the importance of practice.
[285] *Religious Affections*, Yale 2, p. 344.
[286] Ibid., p. 345.
[287] Ibid., p. 357.

religious experience. The tenth sign states: "Another thing wherein those affections that are truly gracious and holy, differ from those that are false, is beautiful symmetry and proportion."[288] A beauty of proportionality is portrayed in the graces and affections of the graciously affected person: "There is symmetry and beauty in God's workmanship. The natural body, which God hath made consists of many members; and all are in a beautiful proportion: so it is in the new man, consisting of various graces and affections."[289] Moreover, a proportionate conjunction of religious sensations is displayed in the affections of the saints: "an holy hope and holy fear go together in the saints . . . In the saints, joy and holy fear go together."[290] This proportioned conjunction of affections is one of the important distinguishing characteristics between true saints and what he and other Puritan preachers termed "hypocrites." He says that "one great difference between saints and hypocrites is this, that the joy and comfort of the former is attended with godly sorrow and mourning for sin."[291]

Hypocrites, however, manifest "monstrous disproportion in gracious affections."[292] These affections can appear to be intense at one time; but their intensity cannot be maintained. Edwards uses several examples from nature to illustrate the difference between genuine and hypocritical affections. Concerning the affections of hypocrites he says:

> They are like the waters in the time of a shower of rain, which during the shower, and a little after, run like a brook, and flow abundantly; but are presently quite dry: and when another shower comes, then they will flow again. Whereas a true saint is like a stream from a living spring; which though it may be greatly increased by a shower of rain, and diminished in time of drought; yet constantly runs . . . Many hypocrites are like comets, that appear for a while with a mighty blaze; but are very unsteady and irregular in their motion . . . and their blaze soon disappears, and they appear but once in a great while. But the true saints are like the fixed stars, which, though they rise and set, and are often clouded, yet are steadfast in their orb, and may truly be said to shine with a constant light. Hypocritical affections are like a violent motion; like that of the air that is moved with winds (Jude 12). But gracious affections are more a natural motion, like the stream of a river; which though it has many turns hither and thither, and may meet with obstacles, and

---

[288] Ibid., p. 356.
[289] Ibid.
[290] Ibid., p. 366.
[291] Ibid.
[292] Ibid., p. 365.

run more freely and swiftly in some places than others; yet in the general, with a steady and constant course, tends the same way, till it gets to the ocean.[293]

In each instance the affections of the hypocrite are disproportionate either in intensity or duration. The affections of the saints, however, are beautiful in their proportionality.

There is another proportionate relation in gracious affections. Edwards states at the eleventh positive sign: "Another great and very distinguishing difference between gracious affections and others is, that gracious affections, the higher they are raised, the more is a spiritual appetite and longing of soul after spiritual attainment, increased. On the contrary, false affections rest satisfied in themselves."[294] There is a proportionate increase in the intensity of religious sensations associated with genuine religious experience:

> The more a true saint loves God with a gracious love, the more he desires to love him, and the more uneasy he is at his want of love to him: the more he hates sin, the more he desires to hate it, and laments that he has so much remaining love to it: the more he mourns for sin, the more he longs to mourn for sin: the more his heart is broke, the more he desires it should be broke: the more he thirsts and longs after God and holiness, the more he longs to long, and breathe out his very soul in longings after God.[295]

Holy affections are like kindling, igniting the soul to burn with greater love to God.[296] True saints are never satisfied with their spiritual condition.

After examining eleven positive signs of genuine religious experience, Edwards devotes the most space to his discussion of the twelfth sign.[297] Edwards states the twelfth sign as: "Gracious and holy affections have their exercise and fruit in Christian practice. I mean, they have that influence and power upon him who is the subject of 'em, that they cause that a practice, which is universally conformed to, and directed by Christian rules, should be the practice and business of his life."[298] Edwards demonstrates how each of the previous eleven signs is related to and fulfilled in practice.[299] At the end of that section he writes, "Thus we see how the tendency of holy affections, to such a Christian practice as has been explained, appears from each of these

---

[293] Ibid., pp. 373 and 374.
[294] Ibid., p. 376.
[295] Ibid., p. 377.
[296] Ibid.
[297] See Smith, *Jonathan Edwards, Puritan, Preacher and Philosopher*, p. 49.
[298] *Religious Affections*, Yale 2, p. 383.
[299] Ibid., pp. 394–397.

characteristics of holy affection that have been before spoken of."[300] He then states the connection between the experience of saving grace and the actualization of grace in practice:

> The tendency of grace in the heart to holy practice, is very direct, and the connection most natural, close and necessary. True grace is not an unactive thing; there is nothing in heaven or earth of a more active nature; for 'tis life itself, and the most active kind of life, even spiritual and divine life. 'Tis no barren thing; there is nothing in the universe that in its nature has a greater tendency to fruit—Godliness in the heart has as direct a relation to practice, as a fountain has to a stream, or as the luminous nature of the sun has to beams sent forth, or as life has to breathing, or the beating of the pulse, or any other vital act; or as a habit or principle of action has to action; for 'tis the very nature and notion of grace, that 'tis a principle of holy action or practice. Regeneration, which is the work of God in which grace is infused, has a direct relation to practice . . .[301]

Edwards writes that "This fruit of holy practice is what every grace, and every discovery, and every individual thing, which belongs to Christian experience, has a direct tendency to."[302]

Edwards' emphasis on the actualization of grace in holy practice is consistent with his philosophy of being. For Edwards (as we noted in chapter 1), all being possesses a dispositional character. All being is related to God's being and disposed to be related to other being. As God's being is disposed to overflow in the actualization of creation, so the dispositional nature of being in general tends towards expression in practice. This is especially the case for the saints, those who have been infused with God's beauty in the person of the Holy Spirit. Through the sense of the heart, the saint is given a new disposition which by its nature tends to express itself in practice. Another way of saying this is that the experience of God's beauty is disposed to become visible in the affections and holy practice of the saints. Or, as Sang Lee states, there is a "rhythm of becoming" in this dispositional nature in the saints towards holy practice. Practice actualizes the saints' new disposition and thereby enlarges their being. Lee writes:

> The result of this increasing dynamic of actuality and increase in the life of the saint can be summed up in this way: For one thing, it means that Christian life is already here and now a communion with God (with the

[300] Ibid., p. 397.
[301] Ibid., pp. 398.
[302] Ibid., p. 399.

divine beauty) and participation in God's own life. A Christian's destiny is now and at every moment an actuality. But at the same time, there is a dynamic thrust toward the future in the sanctification of the saint and of history itself. The saint increases in his or her actuality, and this increase is meaningful even to God since such an increase is a participation in God's own self-enlargement. A Christian does not merely contemplate God's beauty and rest satisfied, but he or she is compelled to build God's Kingdom here in history as well as in the everlasting life to come. And the same Christian engages in this enterprise with assurance and hope since it is God who is directly involved in that same enterprise. Edwards' emphasis upon both piety and practice, therefore, is to be seen as ultimately grounded in the rhythm of actuality and increase in God's own life.[303]

Lee rightly says that there is an inseparable connection in Edwards' understanding of the new disposition effected through the sense of the heart and the expression or actualization of this disposition in practice: "Christian practice, therefore, is the inevitable and direct outcome of the new tendency in the saint's mind and heart... Actual Christian practice brings to actuality the real possibility to which the saint's new disposition is a disposition."[304]

Christian practice, says Edwards, "is the chief of all the signs of grace." He continues, "Christian practice is the principal sign by which Christians are to judge, both of their own and others' sincerity of godliness."[305] Practice is a sign of the genuineness of faith both for the individual and for the community. Practice may help a person gain a sense of assurance of salvation: "the Scripture also speaks of Christian practice as a distinguishing and sure evidence of grace to persons' own consciences."[306] Christian practice is also "a manifestation and sign of the sincerity of a professing Christian, to the eye of his neighbors and brethren."[307] Practice is the way in which genuine faith becomes visible to the community.

Coupled with practice, there must also be profession. Edwards says that practice as a sign does not exclude profession of faith. Rather such a public profession is "supposed" in the corporate nature of visible practice. He says that although

> the Christian practice of professors be spoken of as the greatest and most distinguishing sign of their sincerity in their profession, much

---

[303] Lee, *Philosophical Theology*, pp. 235 and 236.
[304] Ibid., p. 232.
[305] *Religious Affections*, Yale 2, pp. 406 and 407.
[306] Ibid., p. 420.
[307] Ibid., p. 412.

more than their profession itself; yet a profession of Christianity is plainly presupposed: it is not the main thing in the evidence, nor anything distinguishing in it; yet 'tis a thing requisite and necessary in it.[308]

Practice validates the genuineness of the faith professed. The reception of God's beauty in the person of the Holy Spirit, through the sense of the heart, must manifest itself in the outward beauty of the saint's affections and practice. Edwards was not only very much concerned with the spiritual dimensions of faith, he was also greatly concerned with the way in which people lived out their faith, both individually and corporately.

In the treatise on *Religious Affections*, Edwards' idea of beauty plays a prominent role. There Edwards states that through the sense of the heart people actually experience God's beauty. Or, as he says, they become "partakers of God's beauty."[309] This experience results in a new apprehension of divine beauty and a love of that beauty, apart from any self-interest. An apprehension of the beauty of holiness inherent in divine beauty efficaciously attracts the soul to God. All genuine religious affections flow from this experience and apprehension of God's beauty. Indeed, beauty itself, in the symmetry and proportionality of the affections, is one of the positive signs of genuine religious experience. Beauty is manifested in the practice and proportioned affections of the saints.

Edwards' idea of beauty was at the center of his understanding of the nature of genuine religious experience. For Edwards, sainthood involved an experience of God's beauty which made beauty manifest in one's life and affections. It remains for us to examine the role of the idea of beauty in Edwards' case descriptions of those he identified as saints.

---

[308] Ibid.
[309] Ibid., p. 201.

V

Cases of Beauty

In addition to theological analysis, Edwards recommended another method for understanding and promoting the revivals. Consistent with his sensible epistemology and with his approach to preaching, Edwards sought to make theological principles sensible through describing the experiences of particular people. Further, it was in Christian practice that the genuineness of Christian experience was most clearly discerned. Thus, Edwards saw a particular usefulness in describing the experiences of people affected by the revivals. He noted this usefulness, for example, in the *Distinguishing Marks*, where, in discussing the "means" of example, he stressed that there was "a language in actions" which went beyond the impression of written principles.[310] Throughout the corpus of his writings chronicling, analyzing, and defending the revivals, Edwards offered case examples as evidence for the authenticity of the revivals.

A Faithful Narrative

A Faithful Narrative, which was published in London in 1737—the first American edition appearing in 1738—was originally an extended letter. It was written to Boston minister Benjamin Colman and dated 30 May 1735. In it Edwards described the revivals of the mid-1730's which took place in Northampton and throughout the Connecticut River valley. The subsequent published edition was an expansion of that letter to Colman. Indeed even the published version maintained the epistolary form. In both the letter and in published editions Edwards chronicled religious experiences which were primarily corporate in nature. Sometimes the corporate experiences involved a conjunction of corporate religious sensations. For example, regarding Northampton

---

[310] *Distinguishing Marks*, Yale 4, p. 238.

he wrote, "this town never was as full of love, nor so full of joy, nor so full of distress as it has lately been."[311] He said the revivals affected people with a "great sense of their own exceeding misery in a natural condition, and their utter helplessness, and insufficiency for themselves, and their exceeding wickedness and guiltiness in the sight of God." Conjoined with that sensibility was "a lively sense of the excellency of Jesus Christ and his suffering and willingness to save sinners . . . and to have hearts filled with love to God and Christ, and a disposition to lie in the dust before him."[312] In a similar fashion, says Edwards, "many express a sense of the glory of the divine perfections and of the excellency and fullness of Jesus Christ, and of their own littleness and unworthiness, in a manner truly wonderful and almost unparalleled; and so likewise of the excellency and wonderfulness of the way of salvation by Jesus Christ."[313] People had a great esteem for the Scriptures, the preaching of the word, sabbath-keeping and singing God's praises. They even had a greater respect for ministers than they previously had.[314] These corporate religious experiences were described in more detail in the published accounts.

In the published version of *A Faithful Narrative*, Edwards described something of the history and condition of the town of Northampton. He told of the "five harvests" or seasons of revival under the leadership of his predecessor and grandfather Solomon Stoddard. The last "harvest" had ended about eighteen years earlier. Edwards stated that these seasons of harvest were not general awakenings in that most of the townspeople were "very insensitive of the things of religion, and engaged in other cares and pursuits."[315] Edwards noted that there was in 1733 a hopeful sign as young people began to take interest in the things of religion. Then in 1734 there was a religious revival in a neighboring community, Pasconinuet. Also that year the deaths of several people—a young man, a young married woman, and an elderly person—had the effect of causing great spiritual concern, especially in a number of young people. It was in this year that Edwards preached his sermon on "Justification by Faith Alone." The preaching of that sermon, which was a response against his perception of a growing threat of Arminianism, Edwards credited with occasioning the Northampton revivals of the mid-1730's.

As in the earlier unpublished letter, Edwards noted the effects on and affects of the town's population. He wrote that in 1735 "the town seemed to be full of the presence of God: it never was so full of love, nor so full of joy,

---

[311] *Faithful Narrative*, Yale 4, p. 104.
[312] Ibid.
[313] Ibid., p. 105.
[314] Ibid.
[315] Ibid., p. 146.

and yet so full of distress as it was then.³¹⁶ Edwards reported that almost every household was concerned with religion. People sang God's praises with renewed vigor. Young people met to talk of "the excellency and divine love of Jesus Christ."³¹⁷ Edwards also described the revival that spread throughout the county and beyond. He noted in the middle colonies the revivalistic work of William and Gilbert Tennent and Theodore Frelinghuysen.

Along with chronicling these events, in *A Faithful Narrative* Edwards also began a practice which would span a number of years and a number of writings. The practice was that of offering an analysis of the kinds of religious experiences which he observed in people during the revivals. After describing the religious experience of people in general, Edwards offered the religious experiences of two notable converts as evidence for the genuineness of the revivals.

THE CASE OF ABIGAIL HUTCHINSON

The first case involved the experience of a woman named Abigail Hutchinson. Although an adult, she was a young woman who had since died from illness. At the outset Edwards distinguishes her and her experience from any resemblance to enthusiasm. He says that she was from "a rational understanding family: there could be nothing in her education that tended to enthusiasm, but rather to the contrary extreme." Although she had been ill for quite some time, she was not prone to "religious melancholy."³¹⁸ She was, however, a little jealous.

It was her jealousy at the conversion of another woman that began the process toward her own conversion. Edwards says that hearing of the other woman's conversion "stirred up a spirit of envy in her towards this young woman, whom she thought very unworthy of being distinguished from others by such a mercy." Out of this envy there developed in Abigail Hutchinson "a firm resolution to obtain the same blessing." She began earnestly to study the Scriptures, with the intent of reading the Bible in its entirety. Several days later, however, she quit reading the Bible in terror over "an extraordinary sense of her own sinfulness."³¹⁹ Her distress continued to grow over the period of several days. Having been too distressed to attend Sunday services, she resolved to visit her minister (Edwards) on the day after the sabbath. When she awoke on Monday morning, however, she did so with an "easiness and calmness she felt in her mind." Scripture verses came to her

---

³¹⁶ Ibid., p. 151.
³¹⁷ Ibid.
³¹⁸ Ibid., p. 191. The case description covers pp. 191–199.
³¹⁹ *Faithful Narrative*, Yale 4, p. 192.

mind "accompanied with a lively sense of the excellency of Christ, and his sufficiency to satisfy for the sins of the whole world." Such contemplations of Christ filled her with joy. She told her brother that "she had seen (i.e. in realizing views of faith) Christ."[320]

A couple of days later she experienced a conjunction of religious sensations. Edwards writes that "while in the enjoyment of a spiritual view of Christ's glory and fulness, her soul was filled with distress for Christless persons, to consider what a miserable condition they were in." A contemplation of God's attributes seemed to cause her mind to be "swallowed up with a sense of the glory of God's truth and other perfections."[321] Edwards says, "She had several days together a sweet sense of the excellency and loveliness of Christ in his meekness." She spent entire days and nights "in a constant ravishing view of the glory of God and Christ, having enjoyed as much as her life could bear." To Edwards it seemed that "she dwelled for days together in a kind of beatific vision of God." This experience of God's beauty and excellency gave her a new sensibility of God's beauty in nature: "She often expressed a sense of the glory of God appearing in the trees, and growth of the fields, and the work of God's hands." She told her sister that she enjoyed living where she could "sit and see the wind blowing the trees, and to behold what God has made."[322]

She "had great longings to die, that she might be with Christ."[323] It was in her death, due to an illness which made it difficult for her to breathe, that Edwards saw evidence of the genuineness of her faith. Edwards says that she was weak for some time and that she appeared to be near death for three days. She seemed "to continue in an admirable sweet composure of soul, without an interruption, to the last, and died as a person that went to sleep, without any struggle."[324] Edwards writes that through the testimony of her experience—which he read to some of her neighbors and friends—"she was looked upon amongst us, as a very eminent instance of Christian experience."[325]

The Case of Phoebe Bartlet

Edwards' second case study was of a subject very different from the first, for little Phoebe Bartlet was but four years old. Edwards received the informa-

---

[320] Ibid., p. 193.
[321] Ibid., p. 194.
[322] Ibid., p. 195.
[323] Ibid., p. 196.
[324] Ibid., p. 198.
[325] Ibid., p. 199.

tion about Phoebe from her parents. As with the case of Abigail Hutchinson, Phoebe Bartlet had had some affecting conversations with her eleven-year-old brother, who had experienced conversion sometime recently. Phoebe's parents did not believe that she was old enough to understand the things of religion. However, they observed her in such activities as admonishing other children and engaging several times a day in prayers in her "closet." On one occasion her mother heard her pray, "Pray, blessed Lord, give me salvation! I pray, beg, pardon all my sins!"[326] After this particular prayer, she expressed fear that she was going to hell. When her mother tried unsuccessfully to quiet her, Phoebe "suddenly ceased crying, and began to smile." She then said "Mother, the kingdom of heaven is come to me!" Then she exclaimed that three passages from her catechism came to her mind. After a return trip to her "closet" she emerged and declared, "I can find God now!"[327]

She then exclaimed "I love God!" and that she did so "better than anything!" Edwards notes that her older sister asked her where she could find God. Phoebe's answer was "in heaven." She was asked if she had been to heaven. She replied, "No." Edwards is quick to declare: "By this it seems not to have been any imagination of anything seen with bodily eyes." When her mother asked if she were still afraid of going to hell, Phoebe replied, "Yes, I was, but now I shan't."[328] In answer to additional queries by her mother, Phoebe acknowledged that she believed that on that very day God had given her salvation. Further, in answer to a neighbor's questions, she declared that God made her feel better than she had before.

Edwards records that there was a marked change in Phoebe from that time on. That afternoon she appeared "exceeding cheerful and joyful."[329] She evidenced deep concern for the condition of the souls of other children. She longed for the sabbath and was strict in its observance. She said that she loved God's house and loved to hear Mr. Edwards preach. She was greatly concerned over having taken some plums from a neighbor's yard, not knowing at the time that it was wrong for her to do so. She loved texts of scripture, and cried in the night over the love of God and Christ.[330] Edwards ends his case description by noting Phoebe's spirit of charity and that she "manifested a great love to her minister."[331]

In the cases that Edwards recorded in *A Faithful Narrative*, the language of

---

[326] Ibid., p. 200. The record of this case covers pp. 199–205.
[327] *Faithful Narrative*, Yale 4, p. 200.
[328] Ibid., p. 201.
[329] Ibid.
[330] Ibid., pp. 203 and 204.
[331] Ibid., pp. 204 and 205.

beauty played a limited role. In these cases, Edwards described the experience of complex beauty in a conjunction of diverse religious sensations. However, the language of beauty would play a much more prominent role in Edwards' later descriptions of the revivals and in the additional cases he would offer as testimony of their authenticity. The language of beauty was to become a more prominent factor in Edwards' case descriptions beginning with the account of his own conversion experience.

THE CASE OF JONATHAN EDWARDS

Edwards' conversion was described by him, in the vocabulary of his language of beauty, as an experience of divine beauty. This apprehension of beauty, through the sense of the heart, produced in him a new perception of other forms of beauty and a manifestation of beauty in his life and affections. Edwards' autobiographical account, entitled simply "Personal Narrative," serves, therefore, as an important model. The date of the "Personal Narrative" also underscores its importance.[332] Written sometime after 1739, it was penned during the height of the revivals. By then Edwards had published his *Five Discourses on Important Subjects*, including "The Excellency of Christ," in which he linked revival sermons with a graphic portrayal of Christ's excellency in the language of intense complex beauty. Also during this time, Edwards was preparing the series of sermons that would later be developed into his analysis of the psychology of religious experience, *Religious Affections*, in which the language of beauty (as shown in our previous chapter) was of importance. It appears that at about the time he wrote the "Personal Narrative" Edwards began more intentionally to link his understanding of beauty with his articulation of genuine religious experience.

The language employed in describing his own religious experience is also important. Richard R. Niebuhr writes that the "Personal Narrative"

> arrests our attention because it not only tells about the author's religious experience but it does so in a vocabulary and system of ideas that Edwards had carefully developed over a period of years. Consequently we learn from the "Personal Narrative" both a good deal about the qualities of Edwards' "conversion" and mystic communion with God and a good deal about the way Edwards approached the description and interpretation of religious experience.[333]

---

[332] Thomas Schafer places the date as early 1740's. See Schafer's editor's introduction to Yale 13, p. 77, note 6. The precise date cannot be known with certainty. The text of the "Personal Narrative" is taken from Faust and Johnson, eds., *Jonathan Edwards, Representative Selections*, pp. 57–72.

[333] Niebuhr, *Streams of Grace*, p. 18.

The particular "vocabulary and system of ideas" to which Niebuhr points is that of beauty. The "Personal Narrative" was written from the vantage point of one who, having observed others' reception of divine beauty through the sense of the heart, is reflecting on his own reception and experience of gracious beauty. Sang Lee is correct in stating that in the "Personal Narrative," Edwards is describing "his own experience of the beauty of God."[334] It is out of his own experience that the experiences of others can be assessed and attested as genuine. Robert Jenson states that in this document, Edwards "describes the paradigmatic experience." Edwards' own experience became for him a paradigmatic experience for all saints.[335]

The "Personal Narrative" is replete with the language of beauty. There one finds Edwards' account of walking in the beauty of nature, of singing forth God's praises, and of rapture and ravishment of soul. After several introductory paragraphs providing a description of his preparatory pilgrimage toward regeneration, Edwards gives an account of his experience of gracious beauty through the sense of the heart. That experience was occasioned by his contemplation of God's glory and majesty:

> The first instance that I remember of that sort of inward, sweet delight in God and in divine things that I have lived in much since, was on reading those words, I Tim. i. 17. *Now unto the King eternal, immortal, invisible, the only wise God, be honor and glory for ever and ever, Amen.* As I read the words, there came into my soul, and was diffused through it, a sense of the glory of the Divine Being; a new sense, quite different from any thing I ever experienced before.[336]

For Edwards that "new sense" was an experience of beauty, described in the language of beauty, especially intense complex beauty. Complex beauty was significant in Edwards' portrayal of the excellency of Christ. Edwards described diverse, even antithetical, attributes conjoined in Christ's person and work. Similarly, in the "Personal Narrative" Edwards writes:

> I walked abroad alone, in a solitary place in my father's pasture, for contemplation. And as I was walking there, and looking up on the sky and

---

[334] Lee, "Mental Activity," p. 392.

[335] Jenson, p. 15. Although in Edwards' published writings, as we shall see, he presents David Brainerd as the ultimate paradigm for genuine religious experience, and although Edwards no doubt incorporated into his own account what he learned from the testimonies of others, one can still agree with Jenson that the "Personal Narrative" functioned as an important paradigm for Edwards. It is with the account of his own experience that Edwards began more fully to employ the language of beauty in describing genuine religious experience.

[336] "Personal Narrative" in Faust and Johnson, *Jonathan Edwards, Representative Selections*, p. 59.

> clouds, there came into my mind so sweet a sense of the glorious majesty and grace of God, that I know not how to express. I seemed to see them both in a sweet conjunction; majesty and meekness joined together; it was a sweet, and gentle, and holy majesty; and also a majestic meekness; an awful sweetness; a high, and great, and holy gentleness.[337]

Other interpreters of Edwards have noted his use here of the language of beauty. Daniel Shea says that when Edwards "scrutinized his own spiritual 'estate', it was absolutely necessary that he be able to acknowledge a view of God's loveliness and majesty in conjunction." Shea adds, "to express the ideal vision in the 'Personal Narrative', Edwards chose the language of theological paradox over that of sensationalism, although we do hear symmetry and can observe the proportion Edwards maintains through a dexterous manipulation of his terms."[338] Commenting on the above-quoted passage from Edwards' narrative, Sang Lee says:

> God's majesty and grace, the logical consistency of which Edwards could not explain, are now seen in a "sweet conjunction." They are united into one singular whole with its own meaning of being inexpressibly "sweet." The ideas of majesty and grace are still at the forefront of the mind's view. But they are so coalesced into each other that Edwards can speak of the majesty only as a "sweet, and gentle, and holy majesty," and grace as a "high, and great, and holy gentleness." As Edwards wrote in a letter, "(God's) majesty need not terrify us, for we behold it *blended* with humility, meekness and sweet condescension." Edwards can be said to have had a rectified habit of mind which enabled him to hold together the ideas of God's majesty and grace in such a way that the transcendently beautiful union of those seemingly contrasting qualities is made explicit and is immediately perceived.[339]

An important point for our discussion is that the language of beauty, evident in the passage quoted above, is also used by Edwards throughout the "Personal Narrative" related to his experience of the new sense. A careful analysis of the "Personal Narrative" shows that the language of beauty in such concepts as conjunction, harmony, and others, permeates his account.

---

[337] Ibid., p. 60.

[338] Daniel B. Shea, Jr. "The Art and Instruction of Jonathan Edwards' *Personal Narrative*." in *The American Puritan Imagination: Essays in Revelation*. ed. Sacvan Bercovitch (New York: Cambridge University Press, 1974), p. 18. Shea continues, "Through heightened paradox the unawakened reader might be brought to see the same sense of God's natural and moral perfections balanced and intermingled with each other," pp. 168 and 169.

[339] Lee, "Mental Activity," p. 392. The letter to which Lee refers is the "Letter to Lady Pepperell," dated Nov. 28, 1751, and found in Yale 16.

For example, in thunderstorms, which formerly terrified him, Edwards heard "the majestic and awful voice of God's thunder, which oftentimes was exceedingly entertaining, leading me to sweet contemplations of my great and glorious God."[340] Christianity itself appeared to Edwards as a conjunction of "pure and humble, holy and heavenly Christianity."[341] Heaven was viewed as a world of "pure, humble, heavenly, divine love."[342] Thinking about the idea of holiness, which "was ravishingly lovely; the highest beauty and amiableness . . . a divine beauty; far purer than any thing here upon earth; and that every thing else was like mire and defilement, in comparison of it . . . brought an inexpressible purity, brightness, peacefulness and ravishment to the soul."[343] Reading the scriptures became an activity of beauty:

> I had then, and at other times, the greatest delight in the holy scriptures, of any book whatsoever. Oftentimes in reading it, every word seemed to touch my heart. I felt a harmony between something in my heart, and those sweet and powerful words. I seemed often to see so much light exhibited by every sentence, and such a refreshing food communicated, that I could not get along in reading; often dwelling long on one sentence, to see the wonders contained in it; and yet almost every sentence seemed to be full of wonders.[344]

Edwards experienced a conjunction of religious sensations in contemplating his relationship in union with Christ:

> I very often think with sweetness of soul, of being a little child, taking hold of Christ, to be led by him through the wilderness of this world . . . I love to think of coming to Christ, to receive salvation of him, poor in spirit, and quite empty of self, humbly exalting him alone; cut off entirely from my own root, in order to grow into, and out of Christ; to have God in Christ be all in all; and to live by faith in the son of God, a life of humble, unfeigned confidence in him.[345]

He wanted to be "emptied of [himself], swallowed up in Christ . . . emptied and annihilated; to lie in the dust, and to be full of Christ alone; to love him with a holy and pure love; to trust in him; to live upon him; to serve and follow him; and to be perfectly sanctified and made pure, with a divine and

---

[340] "Personal Narrative" in Faust and Johnson, *Jonathan Edwards, Representative Selections*, p. 61.
[341] Ibid., p. 62.
[342] Ibid., p. 63.
[343] Ibid.
[344] Ibid., p. 65.
[345] Ibid., p. 67.

heavenly purity."³⁴⁶ Yet at the same time, conjoined with these religious sensations, Edwards was deeply aware of his own wretchedness as a sinner:

> I have had very affecting views of my own sinfulness and vileness; very frequently to such a degree as to hold me in a kind of loud weeping ... I have had a vastly greater sense of my own wickedness, and the badness of my heart, than ever I had before my conversion. It has often appeared to me, that if God should mark iniquity against me, I should appear the very worst of all mankind; of all that have been, since the beginning of the world to this time; and that I should have by far the lowest place in hell.³⁴⁷

This sensation of wretchedness was further conjoined with a heightened sense of God's grace:

> My wickedness, as I am in myself, has long appeared to me perfectly ineffable, and swallowing up all thought and imagination; like an infinite deluge, or mountain over my head. I know not how to express better what my sins appear to me to be, than by heaping infinite upon infinite, and multiplying infinite by infinite. Very often, for these many years, these expressions are in my mind, and in my mouth, "Infinite upon infinite ... Infinite upon infinite!" When I look into my heart, and take a view of my wickedness, it looks like an abyss infinitely deeper than hell. And it appears to me, that were it not for free grace, exalted and raised up to the infinite height of all the fulness and glory of the great Jehovah, and the arm of his power and grace stretched forth in all the majesty of his power, and in all the glory of his sovereignty, I should appear sunk down in my sins below hell itself; far beyond the sight of every thing, but the eye of sovereign grace that can pierce even down to such a depth.³⁴⁸

Finally, several other similar religious sensations had coalesced in Edwards' experience. He says that while being sensible of his "exceeding dependence on God's grace and strength, and mere good pleasure," and also having a sense of abhorrence at his own self-righteousness, so much so that it was nauseating to him, Edwards was nevertheless "greatly afflicted with a proud and self-righteous spirit."³⁴⁹

The language of this new apprehension is evident throughout the "Personal Narrative." In the same paragraph quoted above, in which Edwards

---

³⁴⁶ Ibid., p. 69.
³⁴⁷ Ibid., pp. 69 and 70.
³⁴⁸ Ibid., p. 70.
³⁴⁹ Ibid., p. 71.

records his own initial experience of the "new sense," he describes his immediate reaction to reading the biblical passage 1 Timothy 1:17. That reaction was a new sensibility of God's beauty.[350] An experience of God's beauty produced a new heightened perception of divine beauty. At another point he writes, "God has appeared glorious to me on account of the Trinity. It has made me have exalting thoughts of God, that he subsists in three persons; Father, Son, and Holy Ghost."[351] Later in the narrative Edwards specifically relates this new perception to the person of God as the Holy Spirit:

> I have many times had a sense of the glory of the third person in the Trinity, in his office of Sanctifier; in his holy operations, communicating divine light and life to the soul. God, in the communications of his Holy Spirit, has appeared as an infinite fountain of divine glory and sweetness; being full, and sufficient to fill and satisfy the soul; pouring forth itself in sweet communications; like the sun in its glory, sweetly and pleasantly diffusing light and life.[352]

The most profound perception of God's beauty was a new sensibility of the excellency and beauty of Christ. This Christocentric perception is mentioned in several places in the narrative. Immediately following the paragraph in which he presents his initial experience of the sense of the heart, Edwards writes these words:

> From about that time, I began to have a new kind of apprehensions and ideas of Christ, and the work of redemption, and the glorious way of salvation by him. An inward, sweet sense of these things, at times, came into my heart; and my soul was led away in pleasant views and contemplations of them. And my mind was greatly engaged to spend my time in reading and meditating on Christ, on the beauty and excellency of his person, and the lovely way of salvation by free grace in him.[353]

The book of Canticles was a favorite of Edwards, in which he took special delight, for that book seemed "sweetly to represent the loveliness and beauty of Christ."[354] In the narrative Edwards writes, "since I came to [Northampton], I have often had sweet complacency in God, in views of his glorious perfections and the excellency of Jesus Christ."[355] Edwards also records:

[350] Ibid., p. 59.
[351] Ibid., p. 68.
[352] Ibid., p. 69.
[353] Ibid., pp. 59 and 60.
[354] Ibid., p. 60.
[355] Ibid., pp. 66 and 67.

> I have sometimes had a sense of the excellent fulness of Christ, and his meetness and suitability as a Saviour; whereby he has appeared to me, far above all, the chief of ten thousands. His blood and atonement have appeared sweet, and his righteousness sweet; which was always accompanied with ardency of spirit; and inward strugglings and groanings that cannot be uttered, to be emptied of myself, and swallowed up in Christ. Once as I rode out into the woods for my health, in 1737, having alighted from my horse in a retired place, as my manner commonly has been, to walk for divine contemplation and prayer, I had a view that for me was extraordinary, of the glory of the Son of God, as Mediator between God and man, and his wonderful, great, full, pure and sweet grace and love, and meek and gentle condescension. This grace that appeared so calm and sweet, appeared also great above the heavens. The person of Christ appeared ineffably excellent with an excellency great enough to swallow up all thought and conception.[356]

A ride on horseback into the woods—again the beauty of nature—provided the setting and the opportunity for the contemplation of Christ's beauty and excellency. Such a context is fitting: for Edwards, the beauty of nature was an image of divine beauty. The sense of the heart gave Edwards a new perception of God's beauty portrayed in nature. It has already been noted that in hearing thunder, which previously terrified him, Edwards now perceived God's "majestic and awful voice," thereby "leading me to sweet contemplations of my great and glorious God." Such contemplations caused Edwards to sing aloud or "to speak my thoughts in soliloquies with a singing voice."[357] Edwards records that on another occasion, while he was recuperating from a serious illness, "the light of day came in at my window, it refreshed my soul, from one morning to another. It seemed to be some image of the light of God's glory."[358] In the description of his profound experience of the conjunction of God's majesty and meekness, Edwards records that this complexly beautiful sensation occurred while he was walking in his father's pasture: "And as I was walking there, and looking up on the sky and clouds, there came into my mind so sweet a sense of the glorious majesty and grace of God, that I know not how to express. I seemed to see them both in a sweet conjunction; majesty and meekness joined together."[359] Edwards continues:

> After this my sense of divine things gradually increased, and became more and more lively, and had more of that inward sweetness. The

---

[356] Ibid., pp. 68 and 69.
[357] Ibid., p. 61.
[358] Ibid., p. 66.
[359] Ibid., p. 60.

appearance of every thing was altered; there seemed to be, as it were, a calm, sweet cast, or appearance of divine glory, in almost every thing. God's excellency, his wisdom, his purity and love, seemed to appear in every thing; in the sun, moon, and stars; in the clouds, and blue sky; in the grass, flowers, trees; in the water, and all nature; which used greatly to fix my mind.[360]

Edwards relates that he would sit at night and gaze up at the moon, or during the day, look up at the clouds and sky. He did so, he said, in order "to behold the sweet glory of God in these things; in the mean time, singing forth, with a low voice my contemplations of the Creator and Redeemer."[361] For Edwards all of nature was aesthetically sacramental in that the entire created realm portrayed the beauty of God.

Through the sense of the heart Edwards perceived divine beauty portrayed in many things. He also saw an increased beauty in many divine things. He writes, "[M]y sense of divine things seemed gradually to increase."[362] He continues, "[T]he soul of a true Christian . . . appeared like such a little flower as we see in the spring of the year."[363] The Scriptures appeared to Edwards with a new beauty:

> I had then, and at other times, the greatest delight in the holy scriptures, of any book whatsoever. Oftentimes in reading it, every word seemed to touch my heart. I felt a harmony between something in my heart, and those sweet and powerful words. I seemed often to see so much light exhibited by every sentence, and such a refreshing food communicated, that I could not get along in reading; often dwelling long on one sentence, to see the wonders contained in it; and yet almost every sentence seemed to be full of wonders.[364]

Farther on in the narrative, Edwards writes, "And I have sometimes had an affecting sense of the excellency of the word of God, as a word of life; as the light of life; a sweet, excellent lifegiving word; accompanied with a thirsting after that word, that it might dwell richly in my heart."[365] The gospel message contained in the scriptures appeared to Edwards to have a special beauty. Edwards says that "the sweetest joys I have experienced" arose from "a direct view of the glorious things of the gospel."[366] The gospel appeared as a beautiful treasure to him:

---

[360] Ibid., pp. 60 and 61.
[361] Ibid., p. 61.
[362] Ibid., p. 62.
[363] Ibid., p. 63.
[364] Ibid., p. 65.
[365] Ibid., p. 69.
[366] Ibid., p. 68.

I have loved the doctrines of the gospel; they have been to my soul like green pastures. The gospel has seemed to me the richest treasure; the treasure that I have most desired, and longed that it might dwell richly in me. The way of salvation by Christ has appeared, in a general way, glorious and excellent, most pleasant and most beautiful.[367]

Ultimately, that which appeared to Edwards as most beautiful—apart from the excellencies of God's being—was the attribute of holiness. According to Edwards, holiness was God's most excellent attribute. He writes, "God has appeared to me a glorious and lovely Being chiefly on account of his holiness. The holiness of God has always appeared to me the most lovely of his attributes."[368] It is important to examine the idea of holiness in the "Personal Narrative," but it must be emphasized that the experience of the sense of the heart gave Edwards a new ability to apprehend beauty. This new apprehension was viewed by him as the first effect of the sense of the heart, and thus a primary distinguishing characteristic of sainthood. Saints perceived beauty in an entirely new way.

As we have seen, the sense of the heart was viewed by Edwards as a profound experience of beauty, which was described in the language of beauty, and which resulted in a new perception of divine beauty. There is one other dimension to the aesthetic character of the reception of the new sense. The experience of God's beauty, through the sense of the heart, is evidenced by the manifestation of beauty in the life of the saint. It has been observed that Christ manifested beauty in a dramatic conjunction of extremely diverse attributes. That same concept was applied by Edwards in his analysis of the experience of the saints. Those who, through the sense of the heart, experienced divine beauty manifested beauty in their lives. Beauty was made manifest in the lives and affections of the saints, individually and corporately. Indeed, the manifestation of beauty was viewed by Edwards as a distinguishing criterion of sainthood. As noted above, the idea of holiness was an important theme in the "Personal Narrative." Edwards perceived God's beauty as residing primarily in this attribute. In Edwards' own experience, nothing was perceived as more "ravishingly" beautiful or more divinely beautiful than holiness:

I remember the thoughts I used then to have of holiness; and said sometimes to myself, "I do certainly know that I love holiness, such as the gospel prescribes." It appeared to me, that there was nothing in it but what was ravishingly lovely; the highest beauty and amiableness . . . a divine beauty; far purer than any thing here upon earth; and that

[367] Ibid., p. 67.
[368] Ibid.

every thing else was like mire and defilement, in comparison of it. Holiness, as I then wrote down some of my contemplations on it, appeared to me to be of such a sweet, pleasant, charming, serene, calm nature; which brought an inexpressible purity, brightness, peacefulness and ravishment to the soul.[369]

The beauty of holiness could very well serve as an interesting and important topic of investigation in Edwards' thought; however, for our purposes, it is important to recognize that for Edwards, the idea of holiness brings together the experiential and practical dimensions of his understanding of beauty. It is in holy Christian practice that beauty becomes manifested. Edwards records that the experience of the new sense produced in him an intense longing to live a holy life: "I felt a burning desire to be in everything a complete Christian; and conformed to the blessed image of Christ; and that I might live, in all things, according to the pure, sweet and blessed rules of the gospel."[370] The phrase "complete Christian" may be considered an example of the language of beauty. It is related to other similar phrases and terms which portray a balanced proportionality of affections in the life of the saint. Here it should be noted that Edwards says that he wanted to manifest, outwardly in his conduct and practice, the beautiful nature of that which he experienced inwardly, through the sense of the heart:

> It was my continual strife day and night, and constant inquiry, how I should be more holy, and live more holily, and more becoming a child of God, and a disciple of Christ. I now sought an increase of grace and holiness, and a holy life, with much more earnestness, than ever I sought grace before I had it. I used to be continually examining myself, and studying and contriving for likely ways and means, how I should live holily . . . I went on with my eager pursuit after more holiness, and conformity to Christ.[371]

Beauty expressed in holiness produced its own beautiful character in the life of the saint:

> [Holiness] made the soul like a field or garden of God, with all manner of pleasant flowers; all pleasant, delightful, and undisturbed; enjoying a sweet calm and the gently vivifying beams of the sun. The soul of a true Christian, as I then wrote my meditations, appeared like such a little white flower as we see in the spring of the year; low and humble on the ground, opening its bosom to receive the pleasant beams of the sun's glory; rejoicing

---

[369] Ibid., p. 63.
[370] Ibid., p. 62.
[371] Ibid.

as it were in a calm rapture; diffusing around a sweet fragrancy; standing peacefully and lovingly, in the midst of other flowers round about; all in like manner opening their bosoms, to drink in the light of the sun.[372]

Sometime after 1739 Edwards penned his "Personal Narrative." He articulated his experience of grace as an experience of God's beauty, in which other forms of beauty were manifested. Edwards' descriptive language in the "Personal Narrative" was an important indicator that he came to view beauty as the very structure of genuine religious experience. For Edwards, anyone who received God's beauty inwardly would manifest beauty outwardly.

Some Thoughts on the Revival

The year 1742 brought James Davenport's "fanatical" preaching tour through New England. In response to Davenport and the revivals in general, Charles Chauncy published that same year a sermon decrying the revivals as an excess of enthusiasm. The title of the sermon was "Enthusiasm Described and Cautioned Against." As a preface to the published version, Chauncy addressed a critical letter directly to Davenport.[373] Also during that year, Edwards preached the series of sermons that would later become his treatise on *Religious Affections*. It was out of this context that Edwards also wrote his, at the time, most ambitious work in defense of the revivals. *Some Thoughts Concerning the Revival* was published the following year.

The Case of Sarah Edwards

After giving a catalogue of the kinds of religious experiences people, young and old, had related to the New England revivals, Edwards, as he did in *A Faithful Narrative*, focuses his description in *Some Thoughts* by giving an individual case study. In *A Faithful Narrative*, he had offered two cases from the Northampton revivals. Here he describes the experience of his wife, Sarah.[374]

---

[372] Ibid., p. 63.

[373] Alan Heimert and Perry Miller, eds. *The Great Awakening: Documents Illustrating the Crisis and Its Consequences* (Indianapolis: Bobbs-Merrill Company, 1967), p. 257. The text of the sermon is found on pp. 229–256. This source also includes Davenport's "Confession and Retractions" on pp. 259–262.

[374] Edwards' account is a rewording of Sarah's own first-person account. Edwards edited the account and here offers a generic case based upon an unidentified individual's experience. Sarah's first-person account is printed in S. E. Dwight's *The Life of President Edwards* (New York: G. & C. & H. Carvill, 1830), pp. 171–186. John B. Carman utilizes Sarah's first-person account in his study of divine polarities. See *Majesty and Meekness: A Comparative Study of Contrast and Harmony in the Concept of God* (Grand Rapids, Mich.: Eerdmans, 1994), pp. 240–246. My purpose in this present study, however, is to examine the descriptive language employed by Edwards in relating Sarah's account.

Edwards had a number of years earlier noted the then Sarah Pierrepont's religious devotion. In his private notes he had written:

> They say there is a young lady in [New Haven] who is beloved of that great Being who made and rules the world, and that there are certain seasons in which this great Being, is some way or other invisible, comes to her and fills her mind with exceeding sweet delight, and that she hardly cares for anything, except to meditate on him—and that she expects after a while to be received up where he is, to be raised up out of the world and caught up into heaven; being assured that he loves her too well to let her remain at a distance from him always. There she is to dwell with him, and to be ravished with his love and delight forever . . . She has a strange sweetness in her mind, and singular purity in her affections; is most just and conscientious in all her conduct; and you could not persuade her to do anything wrong or sinful, if you would give her all the world, lest she should offend this great Being. She is of a wonderful sweetness, calmness and universal benevolence of mind; especially after this great God has manifested himself to her mind . . . She loves to be alone, walking in the fields and groves, and seems to have someone invisible always conversing with her.[375]

Appreciation of Sarah's piety was a characteristic which remained with Edwards throughout their marriage. As he lay dying at Princeton, separated from Sarah, his last words were of her: "Give my kindest love to my dear wife, and tell her that the uncommon union which has so long subsisted between us has been of such a nature as I trust is spiritual and therefore will continue forever."[376]

In the account of her experience recorded in *Some Thoughts Concerning the Revival*, Edwards begins not as he began other cases, by noting a sense of legal or evangelical humiliation in his subject. Here, instead, he describes over several pages a kind of heavenly transport—a rapture of soul focused on the excellency of God and Christ and the beauty of divine things. Of this experience he says that "the soul in the meantime has been as it were perfectly overwhelmed, and swallowed up with light and love and a sweet solace, rest and joy of soul, that was altogether unspeakable."[377] Sarah had a "lovely view

---

[375] Yale 4, p. 68.

[376] Taken from Elisabeth D. Dodds' *Marriage to a Difficult Man: The "Uncommon Union" of Jonathan and Sarah Edwards* (Philadelphia: Westminster Press, 1971), p. 201. Dodds devotes a chapter to Sarah's account entitled "To the Breaking Point and Back." See pp. 95–106. Dodds can't quite decide whether Sarah's experience is the result of religious fervor or mental illness: did she have religious transport or a nervous breakdown? See p. 106. In response, it should be noted that Sarah's experience is in essence consistent with Edwards' accounts of his other case examples.

[377] Yale 4, p. 332. Sarah's first-person account, however, begins with a keen sensibility of her own sinfulness, occasioned by a mild rebuke from her husband. See Dwight, *The Life of President Edwards*, p. 172.

or sense of the infinite beauty and amiableness of Christ's person, and the heavenly sweetness of his excellent love." Her soul "remained in a kind of heavenly Elysium, and did as it were swim in the rays of Christ's love." She had "extraordinary views of divine things, and religious affections."[378] These rapturous experiences were not, however, says Edwards, the result of being in a trance. Indeed, Edwards is careful to distance his wife from the label of enthusiasm, even noting that she was not converted during the recent revivals. Neither was she "converted nor educated in that enthusiastical town of Northampton (as some may be ready to call it)."[379]

The first mention of a sensibility of sinfulness in his wife is described by Edwards as being conjoined with a sensibility of joy and of God's majesty: "This great rejoicing has been a rejoicing with, trembling, i.e. attended with a deep sense of the greatness and majesty of God, and the person's own exceeding littleness and vileness."[380] These religious sensations manifested themselves in Sarah "with a wonderful alteration of outward behavior, in many things, visible to those who are most intimately acquainted, so as lately to have become as it were a new person."[381] The affections became more constant and steadfast, and less subject to vicissitudes. Further, Sarah evidenced a humility and a particular disposition against judging the religious experience of other professing Christians. There was also a keen sense of "the importance of moral social duties" and the necessity of manifesting one's faith in practice.[382] Sarah had "an extraordinary sense of the awful majesty and greatness of God," as well as a sense of God's holiness and wrath, a sense of the misery of sinners, and a "deep mourning for sin."[383] Edwards describes her distinct sensibility associated with each person of the Trinity: God's glory, Christ's beauty and sufficiency, and "a sense of the glory of the Holy Spirit."[384]

Outward affections were also evident: affections such as singing praises to God and deep longings after God and heaven, along with increased awareness of social responsibilities, such as duty to the poor and the encouragement of ministers.[385] Sarah longed for heaven as "a world of love, where love shall be the saints' eternal food, and they shall dwell in the light of love, and swim in an ocean of love, and where the very air and breath will be nothing

---

[378] Yale 4, p. 332.
[379] Ibid., p. 332.
[380] Ibid., p. 333.
[381] Ibid., p. 334.
[382] Ibid., p. 335.
[383] Ibid., p. 336.
[384] Ibid., pp. 336 and 337.
[385] Ibid., pp. 338 and 339.

but love," producing a "sweetness and ravishment of soul."[386] His wife was totally committed to God, says Edwards, with

> a daily sensible doing and suffering everything for God for a long time past, eating for God, and working for God, and sleeping for God, and bearing pain and trouble for God, and doing all as the service of love, and so doing it with a continual, uninterrupted cheerfulness, peace and joy. "O how good," said the person once, "is it to work for God in the daytime, and at night to lie down under his smiles!"[387]

Showing that Sarah was not so heavenly minded that she was no earthly good, Edwards states that

> High experiences and religious affections in this person have not been attended with any disposition at all to neglect the necessary business of a secular calling, to spend the time in reading and prayer, and other exercises of devotion; but worldly business has been attended with great alacrity, as part of the service of God.[388]

Such a sense of God in the business of life was "found to be as good as prayer."[389]

Following his lengthy case exposition, Edwards offers this declaration to critics of the revivals: "Now if such things are enthusiasm, and the fruits of a distempered brain, let my brain be evermore possessed of that happy distemper! If this be distraction, I pray God that the world of mankind may be all seized with this benign, meek, beneficent, beatifical, glorious distraction!"[390]

In describing the case of Sarah Edwards, Jonathan Edwards used again the vocabulary of his language of beauty. The first affections he described in his subject were related to a sensibility of God's beauty and the beauty of Christ and divine things. Beauty was the foundation of all other affections. There was also an experience of a conjunction of religious sensations: for example, God's excellency and personal sinfulness. Sarah's experience could thus be described as intensely and complexly beautiful. Edwards wanted to distinguish her experience from enthusiasm by showing that such religious sensibility produced in her a social awareness. Further, Sarah could experience heavenly transport and rapture of soul and still be grounded in the affairs of everyday life coupled with a steady piety.

Edwards closes this section of the treatise by stating that the experience

---

[386] Ibid., p. 339.
[387] Ibid., p. 340.
[388] Ibid.
[389] Ibid.
[390] Ibid., p. 341.

described in the case was not uncommon throughout the revivals. He says, "[Y]et there is that uniformity observable, that 'tis easy to be seen that in general 'tis the same spirit from whence the work in all parts of the land has originated."[391] In the experiences of Sarah and others, Edwards saw clear evidence of the genuineness of the Spirit's work in the revivals. The experiences of those affected by the revivals—with Sarah Edwards as a case in point—were beautiful.

The Case of David Brainerd

In more ways than one, David Brainerd provided Edwards with his most significant case study in support of the religion of the revivals. As he lay dying in Edwards' home, Brainerd entrusted Edwards with his diary manuscript, as well as other related papers. In these papers the experience of Brainerd as a missionary to the Indians and the experiences of a number of his converts were described. It was Brainerd himself, however, who was Edwards' most significant case. It was Brainerd's own religious experience and relatively brief life, articulated in Brainerd's own words, that Edwards utilized as *the* case for genuine religious experience. Before he wrote *Religious Affections*, Edwards had presented what he thought was *the* case example in the experience of his wife, Sarah, anonymously portrayed in *Some Thoughts Concerning the Revival*. Then, providentially, Edwards no doubt believed that in Brainerd he had the necessary descriptions for an even more dramatic case. Brainerd provided a case that more fully fit, or was shaped to fit, Edwards' theory of genuine religious experience, as explicated in *Religious Affections*. Indeed, Norman Pettit is correct in stating: "Had Edwards deliberately sought out an epilogue to his revival writings, he could not have done better."[392]

Brainerd was also a particularly useful case because throughout Brainerd's ministry he had worked very hard to distance himself from the label of enthusiasm. That label had been associated with him since the time of his expulsion from Yale. Brainerd had criticized the piety of one of his tutors, and was

---

[391] Ibid., p. 342.

[392] See Norman Pettit's editor's introduction in *The Life of David Brainerd*, Yale 7, p. 10. Pettit sees Brainerd as providing a bridge between Edwards' revivalistic writing and his later work. Pettit, however, may be reaching just a bit in seeing Brainerd as the man behind *The Nature of True Virtue*. Pettit is correct in stating that "as spiritual biography the *Life of Brainerd* carried on where Edwards had left off," i.e. with the account of Sarah's experience (p. 8). Pettit writes, "Brainerd looms as the phantom figure in the text" (p. 13). Further, Pettit sees a remarkable degree of resemblance between the conversion accounts of Brainerd and Sarah (p. 8). Although this observation is accurate, it seems to me that there is even more similarity between the account of Brainerd's conversion and Edwards' own conversion account in the "Personal Narrative."

expelled. Brainerd, privately he thought, criticized tutor Chauncey Whittelsey as having "no more grace than a chair."[393]

Since its publication in 1749, Edwards' *Life of David Brainerd* has been his most popular work, having been reprinted more than any other.[394] It is clear from the Yale edition of this work, with Brainerd's manuscript version and Edwards' published version in columns side by side, that Edwards edited material from the manuscript. Among other things, Edwards toned down Brainerd's melancholy spirit and reworded Brainerd's diction. Pettit says that "Edwards omitted those parts of the diary that he disliked, substituted his own summary of them, and at times changed Brainerd's wording."[395] As in his editing of Sarah Edwards' first-person account, Edwards was intentional in his presentation of Brainerd's diary. Edwards wanted to promote the very kind of experiences he was describing. However, in Brainerd's diary Edwards was working with an account of one who had been putting to work the principles of Edwards' understanding of the nature of genuine religious experience. Brainerd applied these principles not only in his own piety but in his missionary work as well. Brainerd had evaluated the experiences of his Indian converts by the criteria in Edwards' *Distinguishing Marks*. Further, according to Norman Pettit, Brainerd intentionally sought to conform to principles Edwards expounded in *Religious Affections* and other works.[396]

Edwards divides *The Life of David Brainerd* into eight parts focusing on particular periods of Brainerd's life. Interspersed throughout are Edwards' editorial comments, either summarizing material he omitted or adding additional comments. Edwards also attached a section entitled "Some Further Remains of the Rev. Mr. David Brainerd," in which he included additional diary entries and correspondence. Edwards concluded *The Life of David Brainerd* with an appendix in which he offered reflections and observations on the significance of Brainerd as a model of genuine religious experience.

It is in the work's preface that Edwards noted the two ways of "representing and recommending true religion," that is, theological precepts and real-life examples. There Edwards commends Brainerd as an "excellent person" who exercised keen discrimination in religious matters "especially in things appertaining to inward experimental religion; most accurately distin-

---

[393] See Norman Pettit's editor's introduction in *Life of David Brainerd*, Yale 7, p. 42. Pettit's statement concerning the usefulness of Brainerd related to enthusiasm is on p. 20.

[394] Norman Pettit's editor's introduction in *Life of David Brainerd*, Yale 7, p. 1.

[395] Norman Pettit's editor's introduction in *Life of David Brainerd*, Yale 7, p. 22. For examples, see pp. 80–84.

[396] Norman Pettit's editor's introduction in *Life of David Brainerd* Yale 7, p. 6. My purpose in this study, however, is not to examine Brainerd's cases, but rather the case of Brainerd.

guishing between real solid piety and enthusiasm."[397] Brainerd was born in 1718. Before his conversion in 1739, Brainerd is depicted as a serious, if not melancholy lad, who at times had "a sense of my danger and the wrath of God."[398] Brainerd said, "I constantly strove after whatever qualifications I imagined others obtained before the reception of Christ, in order to recommend me to his favor."[399] Brainerd said that he heartily pursued salvation to the utmost of his abilities: "Thus, scores of times, I vainly imagined myself humbled and prepared for saving mercy."[400] As in Edwards' account of his own conversion, Brainerd found himself unsettled regarding the doctrine of the sovereignty of God. He wrote: "I could not bear that it should be wholly at God's pleasure to save or damn me, just as he would."[401] Edwards omits a section where Brainerd expresses that he is enraged at God on account of this doctrine.[402] Following his account of Brainerd's wrestling with this doctrine and expressing a lack of spiritual sensibility, Edwards records Brainerd's conversion experience. Brainerd had the experience, he says, on 12 July 1739.

As in Edwards' conversion experience, Brainerd was walking in a solitary spot as a particular passage of scripture, in this case 1 Pet. 1:8, came to his mind. Brainerd experienced the sense of the heart and a new apprehension of God's beauty. Here is the narrative recorded by Edwards, in words closely following Brainerd's diary: "[A]s I was walking in a dark thick grove, 'unspeakable glory' [1 Pet. 1:8] seemed to open to the view and apprehension of my soul."[403] This was not a vision or any enthusiastic revelation, he says, "but it was a new inward apprehension or view that I had of God, such as I never had before, nor anything which had the least resemblance of it."[404] Brainerd said that he stood still in wonderment for quite some time. He said that he "never had seen before anything comparable to [the new apprehension] for excellency and beauty."[405] This view or apprehension was not of any one particular person of the Trinity, but "it appeared to be divine glory that I then beheld."[406] Brainerd records that he was so "captivated and delighted with the excellency, loveliness, greatness and other perfections of God," that he felt

---

[397] *Life of David Brainerd*, Yale 7, p. 92. On the "two ways" of promoting the revivals, see p. 89.
[398] *Life of David Brainerd*, Yale 7, p. 105. Unless otherwise noted, I am quoting from Edwards' accounts not Brainerd's diary.
[399] *Life of David Brainerd*, Yale 7, p. 110.
[400] Ibid., p. 115.
[401] Ibid., p. 124.
[402] Ibid., pp. 125–127.
[403] Ibid., p. 138.
[404] Ibid.
[405] Ibid.
[406] Ibid., p. 139.

"swallowed up" into God.[407] Also, the way of salvation appeared to him with a new excellency.[408] Brainerd says that he continued in the new state of "sweet relish" for several days. However, not long after, he "was again involved in thick darkness and under great distress."[409] This sense of conviction was different from before his conversion experience: "I was guilty, afraid, and ashamed to come before God, was exceeding pressed with a sense of guilt. But it was not long before I felt (I trust) true repentance and joy in God."[410] Following the record of these diverse religious sensations, Edwards omits a section in which Brainerd admitted to having a judgmental attitude toward ministers and people who called themselves Christians but who did not have some kind of experience of grace.[411] Edwards did not want Brainerd to be identified with this practice of some enthusiasts, nor to add fuel to the Yale College incident.[412] Brainerd says that he continued in diverse religious sensations, sometimes darkness, sometimes sweetness, sometimes both. For example, he records that on 18 October:

> In my morning devotions, my soul was exceedingly melted for and bitterly mourned over my exceeding sinfulness and vileness. I never before had felt so pungent and deep a sense of the odious nature of sin, as at this time. My soul was then unusually carried forth in love to God, and had a lively sense of God's love to me.[413]

Consistent with Edwards' account of his own conversion and the case accounts of others, Brainerd experienced a conjunction of religious sensations as an intensely and complexly beautiful experience.

Throughout the account, Edwards portrays Brainerd in similar fashion. For example, as an editorial summary of Brainerd's experience in May of 1742, Edwards writes:

> Through the remaining part of this week he complains almost every day of desertion and inward trials and conflicts, attended with dejection of spirit; but yet speaks of times of relief and sweetness, and daily refreshing visits of the divine spirit, affording special assistance and comfort, and enabling, at some times, to much fervency and enlargement in religious duties.[414]

---

[407] Ibid.
[408] Ibid., p. 140.
[409] Ibid., p. 141.
[410] Ibid.
[411] Ibid., pp. 141 and 142.
[412] Ibid.; see Edwards' editorial comments, pp. 154–156.
[413] *Life of David Brainerd*, Yale 7, p. 147.
[414] Ibid., p. 166.

Edwards again editorializes a later period of the same year. He says of Brainerd:

> In his diary for the next seven days, he expresses a variety of exercises of mind: He speaks of great longings after God and holiness, and earnest desires for the conversion of others, of fervency in prayer, and power to wrestle with God, and of composure, comfort and sweetness, from time to time; but expresses a sense of the vile abomination of his heart, and bitterly complains of his barrenness and the passing "body of death" [Rom. 7:24]; and says he saw clearly that whatever he enjoyed, better than hell, was free grace: Complains of his being exceeding low, much below the character of a child of God; and is sometimes disconsolate and dejected.[415]

Brainerd, more than any other case presented by Edwards, experienced the intensity of diverse religious sensations. Brainerd's experience was, of all of Edwards' cases, the most intensely and complexly beautiful.

Indeed, the remaining record of Brainerd's ministry reveals one who was constantly wrestling with God and struggling with the intensity of his religious sensations.[416] The intensity of these sensations was also affected by Brainerd's deteriorating physical health. For example, Edwards, making editorial comment on Brainerd's condition during November, 1743, states:

> It appears by his diary for the remaining part of the week and for two following weeks, that great part of the time he was very ill and full of pain; and yet obliged through his circumstances, in this ill state of body, to be at great fatigues in labor and travelling day and night, and to expose himself in stormy and severe seasons. He from time to time, within this space, speaks of outgoings of soul after God; his heart strengthened in God; seasons of divine sweetness and comfort; his heart affected with gratitude and mercies, etc. And yet there are many complaints of lifelessness, weakness of grace, distance from God and great unprofitableness. But still there appears a constant care, from day to day, not to lose time, but to improve it all for God.[417]

There is a lengthy section in *The Life of David Brainerd* describing Brainerd's missionary activity in 1745 and 1746. A number of cases of his converts are described.[418] Some of these involved an experience of a conjunction of religious sensations. For example, on 28 October 1745 Brainerd records that

---

[415] Ibid., pp. 171 and 172.
[416] Ibid.; see pp. 84, 190, 194, 204, 222, 256, 261, and 262.
[417] *Life of David Brainerd*, Yale 7, p. 227.
[418] Ibid.; see, for example, pp. 306 and 309, and lengthy sections from pp. 298–428.

"[t]he Word of God at this time seemed to fall upon the assembly with a divine power and influence, especially toward the close of my discourse. There was both a sweet melting and bitter mourning in the audience."[419] In that instance, Brainerd waited several weeks before baptizing the converts, in order to observe and judge the genuineness of their conversion.[420] There was one particular case to which Brainerd referred several times in his diary. For 16 December 1745 he records that a woman came to him in such great agony and apparent distress that "the sweat ran off her face for a considerable time."[421] Then for 22 December he records that the woman mentioned earlier received, along with some others, some spiritual comfort to the extent that he wrote, "I have abundant reason to think she had passed a saving change some days before."[422] She even related to Brainerd that she had some sense of a disinterested benevolence.[423] She appears again in the diary for 9 February 1746, in spiritual distress again. Then on 9 March Brainerd discusses her condition for several pages in language similar to his own conversion account. He even notes the same passage of scripture (1 Pet. 1:8) that was important in his own conversion experience, stating that more than any other person he had ever seen she was filled with "joy unspeakable and full of glory."[424] He described her experience as "sweet and surprising ecstasy" that "appeared to spring from a true spiritual discovery of the glory, ravishing beauty, and excellency of Christ." Her experiences, says Brainerd, did not arise from any sense of self-interest "but from a view of [Christ's] personal excellency and transcendent loveliness."[425] Along with what Brainerd calls this "ravishing comfort" was a "most tender sense of the evil of sin" and a "humbling sense of her own meanness and unworthiness." Says Brainerd, "I then thought I had never seen such an appearance of ecstasy and humility meeting in any one person in all my life before."[426]

In the final section of the diary account, Edwards notes that by late September 1746 the diary was interrupted more often by periods when Brainerd, because of his illness, was unable to record entries. Throughout the closing months of his ministry, Brainerd's illness (he eventually died of tuberculosis) became an increasing handicap. Unable to remain on the mission field, Brainerd spent his final days in Edwards' home. There he was attended by Edwards'

---

[419] Yale 7, p. 335.
[420] Ibid., p. 334.
[421] Ibid., p. 345.
[422] Ibid., p. 346.
[423] Ibid., p. 347.
[424] Ibid., p. 369.
[425] Ibid., p. 371.
[426] Ibid., p. 372.

daughter, Jerusha. Brainerd died on 9 October 1747, at thirty years of age. As in the portrayal of his life and ministry, so also in the account of his dying Edwards portrayed Brainerd as a model saint.

Following an account of the circumstances of Brainerd's death and a section entitled "Some Further Remains of the Rev. Mr. David Brainerd," which included an additional diary entry and several items of correspondence, Edwards attached an editorial appendix entitled: "An Appendix Containing Some Reflections and Observations on the Preceding Memoirs of Mr. Brainerd." In this section, Edwards commented on the special opportunity provided by the example of Brainerd "to see the nature of true religion; and the manner of its operation when exemplified in a high degree and powerful exercise."[427]

Edwards notes in the appendix that Brainerd knew and approved of his treatise *Religious Affections*.[428] Indeed, it was in many of the categories of the positive signs of *Religious Affections* that Edwards recommended his ultimate case study. For example, Edwards notes that Brainerd's conversion was genuine in that it brought a thorough change in nature. It was "a great change and an abiding change, rendering him a new man, a new creature: not only a change as to hope and comfort and an apprehension of his own good estate . . . but a change of nature, a change of the abiding habit and temper of his mind."[429] Edwards notes that Brainerd's conversion was not the result of some type of enthusiastical vision, "but a manifestation of God's glory and the beauty of his nature as supremely excellent in itself."[430] A new sensibility of God's beauty was the ground of Brainerd's conversion. The beauty and excellency of God, Christ and divine things, in and of themselves, was the basis of Brainerd's experience, not any self-love or self-interest: "Mr. Brainerd's religion was not selfish and mercenary: His love to God was primarily and principally for the supreme excellency of his own nature, and not built on a preconceived notion that God loved him."[431] A sensibility of God's beauty produced another form of beauty in Brainerd:

> It appears plainly and abundantly all along, from his conversion to his death, that that beauty, that sort of good, which was the great object of the new sense of his mind, the new relish and appetite given him in conversion, and thenceforward maintained and increased in his heart, was holiness, conformity to God, living to God, and glorifying him.[432]

---

[427] Ibid., p. 500.
[428] Ibid., p. 511.
[429] Ibid., p. 502.
[430] Ibid., p. 503.
[431] Ibid., p. 505.
[432] Ibid., p. 506.

Edwards notes the conjunction of diverse religious sensations in Brainerd's experience. Brainerd's "religious illuminations, affections, and comfort, seemed to a great degree to be attended with evangelical humiliation; consisting in a sense of his utter insufficiency, despicableness and odiousness."[433] Edwards further states, "His joy seemed truly to be a rejoicing with trembling. His assurance and comfort differed greatly from a false enthusiastic confidence and joy, in that it promoted and maintained mourning for sin: holy mourning . . . He was a mourner for sin all his days."[434]

In contrast to the religion of the hypocrites which Edwards described in the eleventh sign of *Religious Affections*, Brainerd's "religion was not like a blazing meteor, or like a flaming comet" or a star. Rather, Brainerd's affections were "more like the steady light of heaven," constant and consistent, even in "retirement and secret places."[435] Also consistent with the criteria explicated in that positive sign, Edwards says that "the greater and sweeter his comforts were, the more vehement were his desires after holiness."[436] Edwards states that, as expressed in the criteria of *Religious Affections*, Brainerd was more concerned with the nature of religious experiences than with a particular order in those experiences.[437] And, as in the criteria for the twelfth and most important positive sign in *Religious Affections*, Edwards said of Brainerd: "All his inward illuminations, affections, and comforts, seemed to have a direct tendency to practice, and to issue in it."[438]

Edwards used *The Life of David Brainerd* to show that "there is indeed such a thing as true experimental religion, arising from immediate divine influences, supernaturally enlightening and convincing the mind, and powerfully impressing, quickening, sanctifying, and governing the heart."[439] David Brainerd was Edwards' ultimate case for affectionate religion. Brainerd's experience was a helpful model for the important task of distinguishing true from false religious experience. Edwards wrote of the importance of that task:

> The want of distinguishing in things that appertain to experimental religion is one of the chief miseries of the professing world. 'Tis attended with very many most dismal consequences: Multitudes of souls are fatally deluded about themselves and their own state; and so are eternally undone.[440]

---

[433] Ibid.
[434] Ibid., p. 508.
[435] Ibid., pp. 508 and 509.
[436] Ibid., p. 509.
[437] Ibid., p. 511.
[438] Ibid., p. 510.
[439] Ibid., p. 520.
[440] Ibid., p. 519.

For such important work, Edwards mustered his best resources. David Brainerd, in his life and ministry and in the record he kept of it, provided Edwards with significant aid in promoting true religion. Edwards burst forth in appreciation for the subject who proved to be his ultimate case, much as he had for his wife's case:

> I say, if all these things are the fruits of enthusiasm, why should not enthusiasm be thought a desirable and excellent thing? For what can true religion, what can the best philosophy, do more? If vapors and whimsy will bring men to the most thorough virtue . . . if it be so, I say, what cause then has the world to prize and pray for this blessed whimsicalness, and that benign sort of vapors?[441]

Edwards eulogized Brainerd in a sermon preached at Brainerd's funeral. The sermon was published before *The Life of David Brainerd* in December of 1747. Based on 2 Cor. 5:8, the sermon was entitled "True Saints, When absent from the Body, are Present with the Lord." After giving a general exposition of the text, Edwards directly related his message to Brainerd in the sermon's "application" section.[442] Edwards described Brainerd as having had "deep and thorough" convictions of sin, together with a "sense of guilt and misery" for sin.[443] This sensibility was attended with proper intellectual views of the supreme glory of the divine Being, consisting in the infinite dignity and beauty of the perfections of his nature and of the transcendent excellency of the way of salvation by Christ."[444] Edwards particularly noted that Brainerd "detested enthusiasm in all forms and operations."[445] He said that Brainerd's "inward experiences appear to have been of the right kind and were very remarkable as to their degree, so was his outward behavior and practice agreeable."[446] As Edwards ended his sermon, he presented Brainerd as a model for "the excellency and amiableness of thorough religion in experience and practice."[447]

Edwards presented David Brainerd to the world as the paradigm of genuine religion.[448] In doing so, he used the language of beauty. Edwards

---

[441] Ibid., p. 521.
[442] This observation is made by Pettit in Yale 7 on p. 543, note #1.
[443] "True Saints, When Absent From the Body, etc," Yale 7, pp. 543 and 544.
[444] Ibid., p. 544.
[445] Ibid., p. 547.
[446] Ibid., p. 548.
[447] Ibid., pp. 553 and 554.
[448] This is certainly the case in Edwards' published writings. However, as has been shown, the account of his own experience described in his "Personal Narrative" was also an important model. It was there that he began more fully to relate the language of beauty to descriptions of genuine religion.

presented Brainerd's religious experience as an experience of God's beauty, grounded on divine beauty itself. According to Edwards, Brainerd displayed complex beauty in the diversity of his religious sensations and in proportioned affections. David Brainerd was Edwards' most emphatic case for the centrality of beauty in his understanding of genuine religious experience.

VI

Conclusion

The language of beauty was an important part of Edwards' thought. It was in the vocabulary of the language of beauty that Edwards expressed his most important theological and philosophical ideas, including his understanding of the nature of religious experience. For Edwards, beauty consisted in various relations of equality, symmetry, proportionality, and so on. These kinds of secondary beauty were perceived in the natural world. Secondary beauty, however, was a shadow of a higher, primary beauty of beings with perception and volition. In primary beauty, the relations were of love, harmony, union, and so on. For Edwards, it was God who was the "foundation and fountain" of all beauty.[449] The triune God was seen to be a society of love and beauty. God's Holy Spirit was beauty. All beauty, indeed all creation, was the overflow of God's inner-trinitarian beauty. Beauty was, for Edwards, the very structure of being.

In Edwards' epistemology, the sense of the heart, as related to religious experience, was understood as an infusion of God's beauty in the person of the Holy Spirit. Through the sense of the heart, one had an actual experience of divine beauty. Beauty was, for Edwards, the structure of genuine religious experience.

This experience of divine beauty became manifested in other forms of beauty. As Christ manifested beauty in his life and ministry in a conjunction of excellencies, saints were to manifest beauty in their lives and affections. Saints were to be "proportioned Christians," evidencing the beauty of proportioned affections. As beauty provided Edwards with an understanding of the structure of being and religious experience, so too was beauty, for him,

---

[449] *Nature of True Virtue*, Yale 8, p. 551.

the structure of genuine community. The church, especially, was to manifest the beauty of love and harmony.

The idea of beauty provided Edwards with a framework for describing genuine religious experience throughout his revivalistic writings. Beauty was one of the important signs of genuine religious experience. God's beauty was the foundation of all genuine religion and affections. It was the experience of divine beauty, through the sense of the heart, by which Edwards defined sainthood. Beauty was made manifest in the saint's proportioned affections. The vocabulary of the language of beauty was clearly present in the account of his own conversion experience in the "Personal Narrative" and in the other case descriptions which Edwards offered in defense and recommendation of the revivals. In those cases, beauty was described as the content and foundation of genuine religious experience. In Edwards' case descriptions his subjects not only experienced divine beauty, they experienced and displayed complex beauty in a conjunction of religious sensations. Further, they acquired a new ability to apprehend beauty; and they manifested beauty in their proportioned affections.

Beauty provided Edwards with a category by which to integrate his thought. According to Conrad Cherry, Edwards' system achieved "the vision of the whole self in a whole world." Edwards achieved "a remarkable balance in his thinking and preaching"; according to Cherry,

> He complemented his didacticism with a sensational shadowing that went beyond moral dictates to direct participation in spiritual truths. He supplemented his pleas for "actual learning" with invitations to a type of knowing in which intellect and affections join in concert. His view of creation, for example, linked all levels of the scale of being into a harmonious praise of God's glory, and his theory of virtue brought into symbiotic relation the beauty of the cosmos, the beauty of human morality, and the beauty of divine benevolence.[450]

It was his idea of beauty, in its full range of theological and metaphysical language, that provided Edwards with the framework for such an integration. For Edwards, beauty was the structure not only of being, but also of genuine religious experience and authentic communal life. For Edwards, being, like beauty, was understood as dynamic and relational. Both were founded upon the dynamic inner-trinitarian relation of God's being. Sainthood involved, indeed was defined by, an experience of God's beauty and the complex beauty of diverse religious sensations, which became manifested in the outward

---

[450] Conrad Cherry, *Nature and Religious Imagination, From Edwards to Bushnell* (Philadelphia: Fortress Press, 1980), p. 62.

beauty of proportioned affections. As in the case of the individual, society, especially the society of the saints, was to manifest beauty in the form of harmony and union.

Edwards pondered beauty in his notebooks. He applied beauty in his sermons and treatises. He related beauty to what he believed to be the most pressing issue of the revivals—the nature of genuine religious experience. The idea of beauty provided Edwards with a category by which to integrate and express his most important philosophical and theological ideas. He expressed those ideas in the vocabulary of the language of beauty. Although the idea of beauty was a factor in the theologies or philosophies of those who succeeded Edwards, none quite achieved his unique integration of nature and theology, of piety and virtue, and of objective and subjective experience. This study has stressed that for Edwards, the structure of genuine religious experience was that of beauty. Genuine religious experience was, for him, an experience of beauty made manifest in beauty. For Jonathan Edwards, the affections of the saints, both individually and corporately, were to be beautiful.

Bibliography

Alexis, Gerhard T. "Jonathan Edwards and the Theocratic Ideal." *Church History* 35.3 (September, 1966): 328–343.

Calvin, John. *Institutes of the Christian Religion. Library of Christian Classics.* Edited by John T. McNeill. Translated by Ford Lewis Battles. Philadelphia: Westminster Press, 1960.

Carman, John B. *Majesty and Meekness: A Comparative Study of Contrast and Harmony in the Concept of God.* Grand Rapids, Mich.: Eerdmans, 1994.

Carse, James. *Jonathan Edwards and The Visibility of God.* New York: Charles Scribner's Sons, 1967.

Cherry, Conrad. *Nature and Religious Imagination, From Edwards to Bushnell.* Philadelphia: Fortress Press, 1980.

Clebsch, William A. *American Religious Thought, a history.* Chicago: University of Chicago Press, 1973.

Delattre, Roland. *Beauty and Sensibility in the Thought of Jonathan Edwards: An Essay in Aesthetics and Theological Ethics.* New Haven: Yale University Press, 1968.

Dodds, Elisabeth D. *Marriage to a Difficult Man: The "Uncommon Union" of Jonathan and Sarah Edwards.* Philadelphia: Westminster Press, 1971.

Dwight, S. E. *The Life of President Edwards.* New York: G. & C. & H. Carvill, 1830.

Edwards, Jonathan. *The Philosophy of Jonathan Edwards From His Private Notebooks.* Edited by Harvey G. Townsend. Eugene: University of Oregon, 1955. Reprint, Westport: Greenwood Press, 1972.

———. *Jonathan Edwards, Representative Selections With Introduction, Bibliography, and Notes.* Edited by Clarence H. Faust and Thomas H. Johnson. New York: Hill and Wang, 1935, revised edition, 1962.

———. *Treatise on Grace and Other Posthumously Published Writings.* Edited by Paul Helm. Greenwood: Attic Press, 1971.

———. *The Works of Jonathan Edwards.* Edited by Edward Hickman. 2 vols. first published 1834. Edinburgh: Banner of Truth Trust, 1974.

———. *The Works of Jonathan Edwards.* General editors Perry Miller (vols. 1 and 2), John E. Smith (vols. 3–9), and Harry S. Stout (vols. 10–22). Vol. 1 (1957), *Freedom of the Will*, edited by Paul Ramsey. Vol. 2 (1959), *Religious Affections*, edited by John E. Smith. Vol. 3 (1970), *Original Sin*, edited by Clyde A.

Holbrook. Vol. 4 (1972), *The Great Awakening*, edited by C. C. Goen. Vol. 5 (1977), *Apocalyptic Writings*, edited by Stephen J. Stein. Vol. 6 (1980), *Scientific and Philosophical Writings*, edited by Wallace E. Anderson. Vol. 7 (1985), *The Life of David Brainerd*, edited by Norman Pettit. Vol. 8 (1989), *Ethical Writings*, edited by Paul Ramsey. Vol. 9 (1989), *A History of the Work of Redemption*, edited by John F. Wilson. Vol. 10 (1992), *Sermons and Discourses 1720–1723*, edited by Wilson H. Kimnach. Vol. 11 (1993), *Typological Writings*, edited by Wallace E. Anderson and Mason I. Lowance, Jr. Vol. 12 (1994), *Ecclesiastical Writings*, edited by David D. Hall. Vol. 13 (1994), *The "Miscellanies" (Entry Nos. a–z, aa–zz, 1–500)*, edited by Thomas A. Schafer. Vol. 14 (1997), *Sermons and Discourses 1723–1729*, edited by Kenneth P. Minkema. Vol. 15 (1998), *Notes on Scripture*, edited by Stephen J. Stein. Vol. 16 (1998), *Letters and Personal Writings*, edited by George S. Claghorn. Vol. 17 (1999), *Sermons and Discourses 1730–1733*, edited by Mark Valeri. Vol. 18 (2000), *The "Miscellanies" (Entry Nos. 501–832)*, edited by Ava Chamberlain. Vol. 19 (2001), *Sermons and Discourses 1734–1738*, edited by M. X. Lesser. Vol. 20 (2002), *The "Miscellanies" (Entry Nos. 833–1152*, edited by Amy Plantinga Pauw. Vol. 21 (2003), *Writings on the Trinity, Grace, and Faith*, edited by Sang Hyun Lee. Vol. 22 (2003), *Sermons and Discourses 1739–1742*, edited by Harry S. Stout and Nathan O. Hatch. New Haven and London: Yale University Press, 1957– .

Elwood, Douglas J. *The Philosophical Theology of Jonathan Edwards*. New York: Columbia University Press, 1960.

Erdt, Terrence. *Jonathan Edwards, Art and the Sense of the Heart*. Amherst: University of Massachusetts Press, 1980.

Fiering, Norman. *Jonathan Edwards's Moral Thought and Its British Context*. Chapel Hill: University of North Carolina Press, 1981.

Gerstner, John H. *Steps to Salvation: The Evangelistic Message of Jonathan Edwards*. Philadelphia: Westminster Press, 1960.

Hatch, Nathan O., and Harry S. Stout, eds. *Jonathan Edwards and the American Experience*. New York and Oxford: Oxford University Press, 1988.

Heimert, Alan and Perry Miller, eds. *The Great Awakening: Documents Illustrating the Crisis and Its Consequences*. Indianapolis: Bobbs-Merrill Company, 1967.

Hoopes, James. "Jonathan Edwards's Religious Psychology." *Journal of American History* 69 (1983): 849–865.

Jenson, Robert W. *America's Theologian: A Recommendation of Jonathan Edwards*. New York and Oxford: Oxford University Press, 1988.

Lee, Sang Hyun. "Mental Activity and the Perception of Beauty in Jonathan Edwards." *Harvard Theological Review* 69 (1976): 369–396.

———. *The Philosophical Theology of Jonathan Edwards*. Princeton: Princeton University Press, 1988.

Locke, John. *An Essay Concerning Human Understanding*. Edited by Peter H. Nidditch. Oxford: Clarendon Press, 1975.

May, Henry F. *The Enlightenment in America*. New York: Oxford University Press, 1976.

McDermott, Gerald R. *One Holy and Happy Society: The Public Theology of Jonathan Edwards*. University Park: Pennsylvania State University Press, 1992.

Miller, Perry. *Errand into the Wilderness.* Cambridge: Belknap/Harvard University Press, 1956.

———. "Jonathan Edwards on the Sense of the Heart." *Harvard Theological Review* 41 (1948): 123–145.

Niebuhr, H. Richard. *The Kingdom of God in America.* New York: Harper and Row, Torchbooks, 1959.

Niebuhr, Richard R. *Streams of Grace: Studies of Jonathan Edwards, Samuel Taylor Coleridge and William James.* Kyoto, Japan: Doshiba University Press, 1983.

Rupp, George E. "The 'Idealism' of Jonathan Edwards." *Harvard Theological Review* 62 (1969): 209–226.

Sairsingh, Krister. "Jonathan Edwards and the Idea of Divine Glory: His Foundational Trinitarianism and its Ecclesial Import." (Ph.D. diss., Harvard University, 1986).

Shea, Daniel B, Jr. "The Art and Instruction of Jonathan Edwards' *Personal Narrative.*" In *The American Puritan Imagination: Essays in Revelation*, edited by Sacvan Bercovitch. New York: Cambridge University Press, 1974.

Simonson, Harold P. *Jonathan Edwards: Theologian of the Heart.* Grand Rapids, Mich.: Eerdmans, 1974.

Smith, John E. *Jonathan Edwards, Puritan, Preacher and Philosopher.* Notre Dame: University of Notre Dame Press, 1992.

Valeri, Mark. "The Economic Thought of Jonathan Edwards." *Church History* 60.1 (March, 1991): 37–54.

Index

affections, 9, 53, 56, 57, 65f, 88, 89, 92, 93, 103, 105, 106, 107
agreement, 4, 5, 6, 7, 26, 50
Alexis, Gerhard T., 44n
Anderson, Wallace E., 20n
apprehension, 22, 25, 41, 66–68, 74, 80, 84, 88, 96, 106
assurance, 61–63, 73,
awakening, 24, 55, 67, 76

Bartlet, Phoebe, 78–79
beauty
  complex, 3, 30, 36, 58, 80, 81, 86, 93, 97, 98, 103, 106
  equality, 1, 6
  general, 9
  intense, 3, 81, 93, 97, 98
  love, 3–4
  moral, 65, 66
  natural, 3–4
  particular, 9
  primary, 5, 8, 105
  secondary, 4–5, 105
  simple, 2–4
  structure of being, 7, 8, 10, 29, 51, 52, 105, 106
  structure of religious experience, intro., 18, 30, 31, 53, 90, 105, 106, 107
being in general, 9, 10, 57, 72
Brainerd, David, 56, 81n, 94–103

Calvin, John, 19
Carman, John B., 90n

Carse, John, 32n
cases, 75–103
Chauncy, Charles, 90
Cherry, Conrad, 106
Christ
  beauty of, 31f, 80, 81, 85, 86, 91, 92, 93, 100, 105
  friend, 39–40
church, 45, 48, 106
Clebsch, William, 31
Colman, Benjamin, 75
concatenation, 41–42
conjunction (conjoined), 3, 23, 26, 34f, 70, 75, 76, 78, 80, 81, 82, 83, 84, 86, 88, 92, 93, 97, 98, 101, 105, 106
consent, 5, 6, 7, 12, 48
conviction, 24, 25, 27, 30, 68, 97

Davenport, James, 90
Delattre, Roland, intro. n, 18n, 32, 33n, 34n
Dodds, Elizabeth, 91n

Edwards, Jonathan (as case), 80–90
Edwards, Sarah (as case), 95–96
Elwood, Douglas, 7n
enthusiasm, 25, 59, 62, 77, 90, 92, 93, 94, 97, 100
Erdt, Terrence, 19
excellency, 1f, 26, 29, 34, 57, 65, 68, 78, 80, 81, 86, 88, 91, 97, 100, 105

experience of beauty, 31f, 55, 64, 65, 67, 74

faculty, 57, 64
Fiering, Norman, 18, 19, 24n
Frelinghuysen, Theodore, 77

Gerstner, John, 25n, 61
glory, 12–15, 18, 81

habit, 18, 21, 28, 58, 64
happiness, 7, 13n
harmony, 2, 3, 4, 6, 46, 48, 82, 105, 106, 107
heaven, 6, 42, 43, 46, 79, 83, 92
hell, 24, 79
holiness, 1, 65, 69, 74, 82, 88, 89, 92
Holy Spirit, 12, 14, 20, 23, 24, 25, 27, 30, 63, 64, 66, 67, 69, 74, 85, 92, 105
honey, 22, 23
Hooker, Thomas, 61
Hooper, James, 18n, 22n
Hutcheson, Francis, 8, 18, 19
Hutchinson, Abigail, 77–79
hypocrite, 61, 69, 70, 71, 101

idea (idealism), 6, 11, 12, 20f, 56, 64, 66
Incarnation, 32
infusion (infused, infusing), 24, 25, 27, 28, 30, 63, 66, 67, 105

James, William, 17n
Jenson Robert W., 46n, 81

Kimnach, Wilson, 20n, 24n, 26n, 27n, 64n
knowledge, 20f, 56, 67
  sensible, 22f, 67
  speculative, 22f, 67

Lee, Sang H., intro. n, 7n, 8, 15, 18, 29, 31, 32, 72, 73, 81, 82
Locke, John, 11, 19, 20, 22n, 31, 56

love, 5, 6, 48, 58, 74, 105, 106
  of benevolence, 9
  of complacence, 9

Malebranche, Niclos, 19
McDermott, Gerald R., 44
millennium, 44–50
Miller, Perry, 19, 20
music, 3, 6, 9, 46

Niebuhr, H. Richard, 44n
Niebuhr, Richard R., intro., 7, 14n, 28n, 80, 81

order, 46f

peace, 48
perception, 7, 8, 28–30, 64, 66, 80, 85–88
Pettit, Norman, 94, 95, 102n
practice, 63, 71–74, 75, 89, 92
preparation, 25, 61, 81
proportion (proportioned, proportionality), 2, 3, 4, 7, 10, 11, 41, 42, 51, 53, 57, 70, 71, 74, 89, 103, 105, 106, 107

Ramsey, Paul, 39, 41n, 46n
religious experience, 15, 17f, 41, 55f, 59, 74, 77, 80, 90, 92, 94, 95, 101, 103, 105–107
Rupp, George, 6n

saints, 15, 25, 27–30, 31, 41, 45, 53, 56, 61–65, 67, 70, 71, 74, 88, 89, 100, 105–107
Sairsingh, Krister, 15
Schafer, Thomas, 7, 80n
sense of the heart, intro., 17, 18f, 53, 64–68, 73, 74, 80, 81, 85–89, 96, 105, 106
shadow, 6, 30
Shaftsbury, Earl of, 19
Shea, Daniel B., 82
Shepherd, Thomas, 61

signs, 20–22, 56
Simonson, Harold, 30
Smith, John E., 17, 18, 56, 57, 65n, 67n, 71n
Stein, Stephen, 51n
Stoddard, Solomon, 76
sweetness, 19, 22, 23, 29

taste, 18, 22, 23, 28, 29, 67
Tennent, Gilbert, 77
Tennent, William, 77

Trinity, 10–12, 13, 31, 32, 40, 45, 92, 105
type (typology), 6, 7, 30, 48

union, 6, 40, 45–52, 83, 105, 107

Valeri, Mark, 53n
virtue, 8, 9
volition, 5

Whittelsey, Chauncey, 95
Wilson, John F., 49n

www.ingramcontent.com/pod-product-compliance
Lightning Source LLC
Chambersburg PA
CBHW050838160426
43192CB00011B/2078